D0560601

praise for *radical alignment*

"Successful communication leads to intentional action, which can only happen with enrollment. This book offers you a breakthrough in finding all three." —SETH GODIN, author of *Leap First*

"*Radical Alignment* offers a simple, straightforward process to start and engage in difficult conversations. Jamieson and Gower have created a structure that actually makes you want to begin the conversations we so often shy away from. By the end of the introduction, I was ready to jump in to the process with both feet. I would recommend this book to anyone looking for an accessible, pragmatic method to becoming a better communicator." —ASH BECKHAM, author of *Step Up*

"As a person who grew up in a household where healthy, collaborative communication was sorely lacking, I can't tell you how much I appreciate this book. As a result of my childhood, it took me decades to learn just the basics of productive conversation and communication in my personal and professional life. Enter Alex and Bob and their All-In Method, which has dramatically changed the way I have conversations forever! *Radical Alignment* walks you through their easy, step-by-step process for having powerful conversations and truly sets you up to become a master communicator. I highly recommend this book if you've struggled to feel heard or understood, and want a roadmap to deepen your connection with the people in your life." —**NICOLE JARDIM**, certified women's health coach, author of *Fix Your Period*, and cohost of *The Period Party* podcast

"If you need to have a difficult conversation, get on the same page, or decide whether or not to move forward with someone or something, this book provides a seamless roadmap so that everything that needs to be said is said and you can feel assured and aligned in your decisions." —**KATE NORTHRUP**, bestselling author of *Do Less*

"Thank goodness for this book. It opens up a new way to communicate with a win-win-win outcome. *Radical Alignment* is a great help to anyone who needs to get on the same page with their partner or team, or create and hold boundaries that support their goals. Essential!" —**JJ VIRGIN**, bestselling author of *The Virgin Diet* and *Miracle Mindset*

"In this marvelous, beautifully written, accessible, and deeply felt book, Alex Jamieson and Bob Gower offer a unique and nuanced perspective on what real conversations entail. In avoiding clichés, they broach a very difficult subject with startling honesty, insight, depth, and clarity. This book will make you ask soul-searching questions about any relationship you want or have. I highly recommend it to anyone who is tired of the ordinary and/or looking to take their relationships to the next level. And I would recommend it to anyone within an organization who is truly invested in meaningful collaboration." —**SRINI PILLAY, MD**, Harvard-trained psychiatrist, brain researcher, certified master executive coach, and author of *Tinker Dabble Doodle Try: Unlock the Power of the Unfocused Mind*

"Diversity, Equity, and Inclusion are about so much more than hiring and compensation. It's about changing the way teams and individuals interact so we are able to truly hear each other and benefit from the variety of perspectives at the table. Too often in my work I see leaders and organizations neglect this crucial aspect of DEI. In this accessible and readable book, Alex and Bob provide a simple set of tools that will help you and your team align and thrive." —**JENNIFER BROWN**, founder and CEO of Jennifer Brown Consulting and author of *How to Be an Inclusive Leader*

"Alex and Bob have incredible insight into the human mind and how different people communicate—so it's no surprise that their writing is incredibly clear and helpful. Their methodology for improving people's alignment at work and in life will change the way you think forever." —**SHANE SNOW**, bestselling author of *Dream Teams*

"So many of the challenges we face in our work—and personal lives—come down to people misunderstanding each other. Bob and Alex have created a powerful framework to help us bridge this divide." —**JOSH SEIDEN**, author of *Outcomes Over Output*

"I sat down to read *Radical Alignment* this weekend, and am I ever glad. Bob Gower and Alex Jamieson have written a terrific guide for having hard conversations—digestible, usable, and welcoming. *Radical Alignment* provides a clean structure that ensures our messiest conversations can be productive." —**GARY BAGLEY**, executive director of New York Cares

"Magic happens when groups of people harness their intention and strengths for a common goal. And *Radical Alignment* helps you do just that." —**TINA ROTH EISENBERG**, founder of CreativeMornings and CEO of Tattly

"The quality of your empathy directly correlates to the quality of information you can gather, and the resulting quality of decisions you make. Understanding people's challenges, intentions, and often conflicting goals will enable you to create high-performing teams and better collaborations. This book with show you the way." —**BARRY O'REILLY**, business advisor, author of *Unlearn* and *Lean Enterprise*, and founder of ExecCamp

Radical Alignment

radical
alignment

**How to Have Game-Changing Conversations
That Will Transform Your Business and Your Life**

Alexandra Jamieson and Bob Gower

sounds true
BOULDER, COLORADO

Sounds True
Boulder, CO 80306

© 2020 Alexandra Jamieson and Bob Gower

Foreword © 2020 Rebekah Borucki

Sounds True is a trademark of Sounds True, Inc.

Published 2020

Cover design by Jennifer Miles
Book design by Gopa & Ted2, Inc.

Printed in Canada

Library of Congress Cataloging-in-Publication Data

Names: Jamieson, Alexandra, 1975- author. | Gower, Bob, 1965- author.
Title: Radical alignment : how to have game-changing conversations that
will transform your business and your life / Alexandra Jamieson,
Bob Gower. Description: Boulder : Sounds True, 2020. |
Includes bibliographical references.
Identifiers: LCCN 2019052880 (print) | LCCN 2019052881 (ebook) |
ISBN 9781683646051 (hardback) | ISBN 9781683646068 (ebook)
Subjects: LCSH: Social interaction. | Comprehension. | Empathy. | Trust.
Classification: LCC HM1111 .J36 2020 (print) | LCC HM1111 (ebook) |
DDC 302—dc23
LC record available at https://lccn.loc.gov/2019052880
LC ebook record available at https://lccn.loc.gov/2019052881

10 9 8 7 6 5 4 3 2 1

To Laken.
May your conversations continue
to change the world.

contents

foreword

TALKING IS A BIG PART of what I do for a living. On video, on social media, in books—I spend most of my day engaging with other people, most of whom I don't know and will never meet in real life. A lot of what I talk about spotlights social justice issues, such as racial and gender inequality and mental health awareness. These discussions can be tricky, especially with strangers, but I feel a deep commitment to having them. The success of these conversations—success meaning an encounter in which both parties learn something and leave feeling heard and respected—is so important to me. To my regret, I spent a lot of years having unsuccessful conversations. I would leave them feeling frustrated, angry, or sad because there was more time spent digging in, defending, and deflecting than having a meaningful exchange of ideas.

These negative interactions weren't limited to my work life. I wasn't showing up as the greatest communicator at home either. I would mean well—inviting my husband or one of my kids to talk about something that had been on my mind and that concerned them—but the conversation would quickly turn into a heated debate in which one person tried to win (that person usually being me) and the other person felt attacked. I was so desperate to get my point across that I was coming off like a tyrant instead of someone who loved them and had their best interests in mind. These failed attempts felt terrible and like I was moving backward in my relationships.

These crises of communication ended the minute I learned about the All-In Method (AIM) from my dear friend Alex, the coauthor of this book you're reading now. "Bob and I have been working on something—tell me what you think," she said. We were in one of our Mistressmind sessions (as Alex called them), daylong roundtables with a few of our closest women friends in which we would discuss business, family, and all the things that light us up (and keep us up at night).

Alex presented a bullet-point version of their method, and I furiously transcribed her words in my notebook. I knew the method was something special before I even put it into practice. And soon, when I finally got to test it out for the first time with my husband, I knew it was a tool I couldn't live without. AIM has not only been a game-changer in my marriage—creating an intelligent framework for negotiations about everything from money to sex to who's doing what chore—it's changed the way I engage with my kids, my friends, and everyone else I love. And it's changed the way they go out and engage with the world.

However, the real magic of this method for me is that it doesn't require two knowing participants to make it work. If just one person understands how to apply it, the interaction benefits all involved. Following the steps of the method has taught me how to communicate all my ideas better, even in "one-sided" conversations. My social media posts, videos, and articles became more effective, reaching more people and resonating more deeply—exactly what I want most as an advocate and activist who wants to make change in the world. Today, I share this method with my family, friends, coaching clients, and online audience. It's one of my all-time favorite personal excellence tools.

AIM elevated the way I show up and serve. I already knew how to talk—I've been yapping away and sharing my big ideas for forty years. Alex and Bob's method taught me how to communicate. And now I'm so excited that you get to experience its magic for yourself!

Rebekah Borucki
Author, meditation guide, and mother of five

introduction

CAN A CONVERSATION CHANGE YOUR LIFE? HELL, YES. ESPECIALLY *THIS* CONVERSATION.

LEARNING HOW TO TALK about tough topics, in a constructive way, is one of the most valuable things we can do as human beings. This book describes a simple, yet powerful, conversation that will help you build the relationships, and the life, that you want.

We believe passionately that the world needs more aligned teams, organizations, communities, families, and intimate partnerships. This means we need people able to have powerful and clear exchanges that build better connections.

With this book, we offer you a tool to help clear away obstacles and help bring your projects, and relationships, to life. We want to help you be a catalyst for positive change by mastering the All-In Method (AIM)—a tested technique that reliably creates an enthusiastic common cause with others.

Conversation is one of the most basic human activities at work and at home. It brings us into close contact with people's complexities and their vulnerabilities. What we've seen through our work with countless organizations, teams, and

individuals is that important conversations are often ineffec-
tive and unproductive, or not even taking place.

What's missing is not alignment per se—people are often
mostly aligned in what they want from an experience. What's
missing is a shared and explicit understanding and empathy
for the nuances of each other's positions. So, conflict devel-
ops when it doesn't need to. What's needed is a framework
to direct our thoughts, words, ears, and heart so that we stay
connected to the reason for our connection.

We live on the third floor of a brownstone in Brooklyn and
often keep our bedroom window open in the spring and fall.
One day, we noticed cigarette smoke wafting into our bedroom and were angered by the insensitivity of our first-floor
neighbors—whom we don't know very well and whom we
think of as being young and irresponsible.

The next day, we found out it was really our second-floor
neighbor smoking on his fire escape below our window. We
know him well—we barbeque together on the roof deck, and
our kids often play together.

Our anger at the first-floor neighbors didn't morph into
anger at the second-floor neighbor when we found out who
the real culprit was. Instead, our anger evaporated completely.

This is the power of empathy.

Our existing relationship with the second-floor neighbor
—and understanding of his challenges, intentions, and
goals—meant that we were able to see beyond any imagined

slight and assume positive intent on his part. We like him, know him, and feel respected by him.

It's this power of empathy we want to see more of in our communities, on our business teams, and in all of our relationships. And through AIM, your conversations will become effective, compelling foundations on which to build new ways of interacting and growing these partnerships.

We are sharing this tool with you because we want you to be able to build empathy and deeper alignment, on demand, in your most important relationships.

For the past nineteen years, Alex has worked as a coach for women, helping them to achieve a better relationship with food and their bodies. Initially, her focus was on what to eat and how to eat it. But it proved challenging to stay in that narrow spot.

Food touches so many parts of our lives, and we can't discuss it without also delving into intimate relationships, career, family, and personal values. Alex increasingly found herself helping people make positive holistic changes in their lives.

Through Alex's work, we came to appreciate the power of being strategic about creating the structures and systems that support you as an individual.

For the past fifteen years, Bob has focused on building better business organizations. His particular concern is helping to create more engagement and collaboration on their teams. He's worked with startups, Fortune 100 companies, and nonprofits spanning a diverse set of industries, including media, health care, energy, banking, insurance, and technology.

He's seen how the demands of the knowledge economy require higher levels of creativity and collaboration at work, but most management systems are built, at best, to create compliance.

Through Bob's work, we came to appreciate that creating truly engaged and collaborative organizations means developing structures and systems that allow people to bring more of their personal selves to work.

These two interlocking forces—being more strategic and tactical personally and bringing more humanity to our professional lives—drive this book.

The technique this book describes was developed for a couple's workshop we taught together and was almost an afterthought. We were searching for a way to support couples in having difficult conversations proactively.

Our thesis was, and is, that if you can have rich conversations before you hit trouble, you'll not only avoid blowups but also you can often create what we call *radical alignment*—a sense of being fully in tune with the person you're relating to.

When you begin with a sense of deep alignment and have a nuanced understanding of, and empathy for, the other people involved, you will not only avoid arguments but also you'll be able to see opportunities previously invisible. When you reduce unnecessary interpersonal friction, you unlock the true potential of teams.

The technique we developed is called AIM. In the ten years since we first taught the technique, it has become the single-most valuable tool in our kit. We use it regularly in both our personal and professional lives and teach it at every opportunity.

The core idea is that when embarking on a new experience (couples moving in together, sales negotiations, asking for a raise, vacation planning, and more), we examine together our individual

- intentions (our personal why, which is connected to our values),
- concerns (things we fear might keep this experience from going well),
- boundaries (our personal non-negotiables), and
- dreams (our hopes and highest aspirations for the experience).

It's the most popular tool we've taught in our respective careers, and we both frequently receive messages or phone calls from friends and clients (often at odd hours when something particular has come up for them) asking us to clarify the steps and review how to use the technique in different circumstances.

Bob once spent an hour during a cab ride in New York going over the conversation steps with a friend in Los Angeles. It helped the friend navigate a new relationship and, after the ride, the taxi driver thanked Bob profusely and told him how much he'd learned by eavesdropping.

Another time, Alex went over the whole conversation in her women's networking group. A month later, one of her friends from the group reported that it had changed the trajectory of her marriage and had gotten her and her husband out of a really rough spot.

Although we might have been a bit slow to realize how valuable this practice can be, its pull has become undeniable. People have been asking us to write this book for five years, and we've finally set aside time to do it. It just feels too important to keep to ourselves.

Although we first imagined this book for a business audience, we quickly realized this was too narrow. We, and the people we've taught it to, have consistently used AIM to create wins in our personal lives as well as our professional lives. It is a simple, guided conversation that can be used to talk about pretty much anything—big or small. We have used it

- ▶ in setting agendas for company retreats and conferences,
- ▶ to create new products and programs,
- ▶ before we go on vacation,
- ▶ during our vacation when unexpected complications arise,

- ▶ with executives launching large, expensive initiatives,
- ▶ in selling million-dollar consulting projects,
- ▶ with small teams at the beginnings of new projects,
- ▶ to deal with difficult relationship issues,
- ▶ with our young son as he navigated the complexities of school and life, and
- ▶ before and during stressful family visits.

We even used it when we decided to get married and planned our wedding. We credit the technique with making that experience as joyful and low drama as possible. In fact, through the conversation, we discovered and adopted high joy and low drama as our core design principles for the experience.

This book is designed to give you everything you need to have the conversation, either with other people who know how AIM works or by yourself for getting personal clarity. It leads others forward powerfully even if they don't know you're using the structure.

We begin the book with insights into how we fall into traps of poor communication and how to strengthen our skills of curiosity, creativity, and listening. A deep dive into the value of emotional intelligence, psychological safety, and diversity of opinions sets us up to become master communicators, a treasured skill set in today's hyperconnected world.

After exploring these foundations, we will walk you through AIM. From preparing yourself and others to set the stage to learning some conducive frameworks for listening, you'll have everything you need to be a powerful facilitator in your life and your work. Soon you'll be using this method with ease, leading those around you to win-win results.

Next, we demonstrate the many uses of AIM with examples, scripts, and suggested closings. Through your intentions, concerns, boundaries, and dreams, the clarity you reach either with partners or alone, at home and at work, will be invaluable.

Finally, we end with additional materials to help you navigate and, we hope, avoid common pitfalls and obstacles to your clarity. You can prepare yourself or a group with the cheat sheet in the appendix to this book.

How to Use This Book

We have written this book to be used as a tool. Our intention is that after reading it, you will be able to use AIM in high-stakes personal and professional interactions and perhaps even facilitate it for others.

Chapters 1–4 introduce the mindset and skills necessary to use the method effectively. They are designed to help you understand the value of structured conversations like this, why they work, and the situations in which you can use them.

Chapters 5–7 walk through AIM itself. If you have an immediate need and want to use the method, feel free to jump ahead to these chapters. These are also chapters you could ask someone to read before you use the method with them.

Chapters 8–10 provide specific examples of where and how to use the conversations, both at work and at home, and describe common problems we've seen people have with the method—and how to handle them.

Learning a type of conversation from a book can be challenging. Things that seem clear and simple on the printed page can become confusing and ambiguous in practice. Challenges like this are a part of the learning process, and each time you use the method it will become more clear what works and what doesn't. For this reason, we encourage you to jump in, try the conversation, and revisit the book as needed.

We also provide a cheat sheet and resources and further reading section at the back of the book, along with additional materials on our website to help you gain facility with the method. We've been using it for almost a decade and still learn something new almost every time we use it. This book is just a starting point for what can become a lifelong practice!

the foundations of great communication

"THE GREAT ENEMY OF COMMUNICATION, WE FIND,
IS THE ILLUSION OF IT."
—WILLIAM H. WHYTE

BACK IN THE 1980S Alex's dad, Jim, used to play chess with a man in the Union of Soviet Socialist Republics (USSR; now Russia). They would mail each other one move at a time on preprinted cards, and their games could take months, or even years, to complete.

During one game, Jim did not hear back from his chess buddy for almost two months and sent a letter asking if anything was wrong. A week or so later he received a letter back with his partner's next move and a simple note saying, "I thought it was your turn."

Communication is foundational to great relationships, and great relationships are essential to success and happiness in life. But too often even simple exchanges go wrong—and with far more impact than a delayed chess game.

In this chapter we want to introduce you to the foundations of great communication. Although the main focus of this book is a specific conversational structure we call the

All-In Method (AIM), success with any communication or conversational tool depends on how you approach using it.

Communication is too often misunderstood to mean either persuasion or sharing—convincing someone of your perspective or simply informing them of it. But communication is so much more than that. It is a deeply embedded human superpower that depends both on sending and on receiving information. And even more than that, great communication means each party in the exchange is changed by it.

THE HUMAN SUPERPOWER

Famed biologist E. O. Wilson notes that humans are a uniquely hypersocial species—more similar in some aspects of our behavior to hive insects than to other primates. He goes on to say that communication is an essential feature of our species—from written language to creation myths to telecommunications, our ability to communicate sets us apart.

Alone, humans are not formidable, but in groups we dominate the planet and affect its climate, geography, and biodiversity. We are a force of nature and a powerful one at that. This is because of group behavior, not our individual behavior. And effective group behavior requires communication.

Because groups are so evolutionarily important to humans —to our survival and dominance—the groups in which we participate individually play an essential role in our personal well-being. This includes our levels of happiness, the length of our lives, and our ability to accomplish personal goals. Further, being socially ostracized or romantically rejected causes our brains to experience pain that feels as real as physical pain. As parents of a middle-school student, we even experience this social pain vicariously!

Although even poorly functioning groups can make big things happen, we also want to be in groups that not only do great things but also provide great experiences for us as individuals.

How well groups achieve their goals (efficiency and effectiveness) and how pleasant the experience of being in the group is (culture and level of relationship) depend largely on the quality of communication in that group. Much, if not most, communication happens in the form of conversations. Back-and-forth exchanges can be enriching and vexing; a source of meaning, intimacy, and pleasure and also of frustration, confusion, and pain.

At home conversations can easily fall into rote and uninspiring patterns.

We ask, "How was your day?" and get a one-word response, and over time our exchanges become primarily functional in nature, focusing on bills, groceries, school schedules, the next meal, or the next vacation. But we humans long for contact and intimacy with each other—almost everything significant in our lives happens with, or because of, other people.

At worst, ongoing interactions can become abusive and the source of profound dysfunction and emotional pain.

Couples and families can even become what psychologists call *conflict habituated,* a state in which every interaction is approached as a battle for dominance rather than an opportunity for connection and realness.

In our professional lives, we want to work at companies with good cultures that minimize frustration and bring out the best in us. We want jobs that encourage and develop us as human beings. Nowhere is culture more apparent than in the conversations we call meetings. And meetings are the object of scorn and frustration in workplaces around the world.

Meetings are conversations. They might sometimes feel like lectures (or prisons), but, ideally, they are opportunities for people to connect, align with each other, and move forward. They can even be opportunities for profound connection.

Bob has been facilitating work meetings for well over two decades—and it's now his main professional activity, when he's not writing or speaking. He's seen meetings go so wrong that arguments flair and become so intense people almost come to blows or simply walk out. He's also seen people well up with tender emotions so profound that everyone else is brought to tears. All this at work!

More commonly, he's seen people check out—quit emotionally but still show up to work each day—and meetings drag on into a kind of gray haze day after day and week after week of updates, pitches, and order giving.

Our lives and our well-being are connected intimately to the people we interact with and how we interact with them. If we want to improve our lives, there is no better place to start than with our relationships, and relationships start (and end) with conversations—or a lack thereof.

This book is about being deliberate in how we interact with each other—in how we converse. We hope after you read it, you not only have new tools to use but also come to see each interaction you have each day as an opportunity to either get busy living or get busy dying (to paraphrase *The Shawshank Redemption*).

Steve Jobs used to look at himself in the mirror each morning and ask himself: If this was the last day of his life, would he want to do what he was doing that day? If the answer was no too many times in a row, he realized it was time to make a change. We find that asking ourselves a few questions like this before conversations can help us be fully present and can even lead to profound insights into the meaning, purpose, and impact of our lives. One day will be our last day, and one moment our last moment; being fully present for each is a good way to get ready for the last.

At home, poor communication often leads to unnecessary conflict that destabilizes our relationships and turns sources of support into sources of anguish. When we are in regular conflict with our partner, we might even begin to anticipate a clash in every interaction and start avoiding them.

Emotional clashes become habitual not only in our relationships but also in our nervous systems. This neurological loop can cause physical symptoms such as elevated heart rate and blood pressure, symptoms of anxiety. In this way, poor communication can shorten the duration not only of our relationships but also of our lives.

Many people have come to expect conflict at work. Condescending bosses, indifferent colleagues, and micromanagers are so common they have become clichés. Is it any wonder that only 34 percent of employees are fully engaged in their work, and 17 percent are actively disengaged—meaning they work against the objectives of their employer?[1]

Communication, no matter how excellent, will not prevent fundamental misalignments in values and goals, but too often we've seen poor communication allow for conflict to arise when none need exist.

One common culprit is the missing conversation—a conversation we should have had but didn't because we either thought it was self-evident or we did not have the courage or the opportunity to have it.

These missing conversations can hide emotional landmines that, when we stumble upon them later, blow up in our faces. Sometimes the conversation that's missing is some form of a breakup: "I quit," "You're fired," or "I'm leaving you." But more often than not, the needed conversation is one that helps develop a deeper and more nuanced understanding of the other people involved.

We don't need to agree about everything in order to connect with someone. In fact, our differences enrich our lives and relationships. Diversity in gender, sexual orientation, cultural background, and other characteristics statistically improve team performance. In this world of social-media flame wars, cancel culture, and diversity challenges in the workplace, we see a need for more conversations designed to appreciate differences and then find alignment.

The conversation structure outlined in this book, AIM, is a step-by-step process that creates a context for thorough communication, prevents missing conversations, and creates the conditions needed to reach alignment. It is designed to help you be a better communicator by helping you have more thorough and constructive interactions so you can avoid missing essential conversations. It also helps you have these conversations early in a project or a relationship, when changes in trajectory are easier to make.

Our goal is to help you be more thorough, kind, and courageous in your communication. This will help prevent conflict before it starts by exposing potential misalignments early, giving you the time and mental space to mitigate or course correct before investing too deeply in a relationship or in a project. People believe that the more deeply we invest in a certain direction, the more resistant it becomes to change—the so-called sunk-cost fallacy.

The overarching intention of this book, and our work, is to help you to be more deliberate in your relationships. Much of our individual and collective life is driven by habits. These patterns are subconscious and can be valuable time savers, but they are also challenging to change because they are so ingrained—often from childhood and our families of origin.

In groups, these patterns show up as the culture of that group—"how we do things around here." Among individuals, they show up as personal idiosyncrasies and capabilities. For these patterns to change, they need to be interrupted and given the opportunity to shift.

In the following sections, we'll look at some common communication missteps as well as the skills, capabilities, and mindsets of great communicators.

A Taxonomy of Poor Communication

In our experience as coaches and facilitators, poor communication usually falls into one of the following categories.

Misunderstanding

People often have different styles of sharing information as well as different needs when it comes to hearing and learning new information.

Numerous theories and frameworks attempt to sort people into different kinds of communicators. These include personality typologies such as Myers-Briggs and the Enneagram; learning styles such as visual, auditory, relational, or kinetic (VARK); attachment theory, which focuses on individual patterns that often form in early childhood and affect the relationships and bonds between people later; and even disciplines such as astrology, human design, and neurolinguistic programming (NLP).

We are not here to advocate for, or explain, any specific typology. We've found both value and limitations in each of those listed above and more. But we do want you to appreciate that your style and needs will be different than the style and needs of the people you want to communicate with. Misunderstandings often arise when we are communicating in a way that is comfortable and familiar to us but out of sync with our counterparts.

Because of our differences in style, often what we intend to communicate might not be what the other person receives. We might ask a simple question such as, "Did you get a haircut?" and the other person will hear, "I don't like how your hair looks!" The problem is not with either party but in a missing shared context.

Misunderstandings often appear to be disagreements, but the mismatch is in the style of communication, not the intended substance of the communication. Correcting misunderstandings is usually a simple task that requires listening and curiosity. Using AIM and making small communication adjustments, people can share new information more easily and clearly, and they can get their ideas across better.

Emotional Misalignment

Communication is more than just talking to, or at, each other. And it isn't just about being able to more accurately present information to each other. Misunderstandings happen when information is misinterpreted, but much of what we communicate is not only data but also our intentions and how we feel about our counterpart and the topic.

When one person feels disrespected, manipulated, taken advantage of, or disregarded, tension or conflict will usually be the result. Likewise, when a person feels respected, listened to, and considered, even profound disagreements can lose their power. We become more generous with people we like, who we think care about us.

At work, teams with healthy emotional landscapes tend to perform better because they are able to both disagree and commit. In families and romantic partnerships, when having conversations about important topics, it is invaluable to know how people are feeling both in the moment and about the topic to be discussed before even starting.

Topic Creep

If you have ever been in a conversation you thought was about one thing—the next family vacation or the coming product release schedule, and it veers into wildly different territory—disappointment with the honeymoon you had fifteen years ago or hiring needs for the coming quarter—you've experienced topic creep.

Sticking to a single topic and agenda is usually what creates forward momentum. But topic creep can also indicate that the topic wasn't properly framed in the first place or that there is misunderstanding or emotional misalignment.

Attributes of a Good Communicator

Over the years we've noticed that some people tend to be better communicators and that these people share certain attributes—the first and most important of which is the intention to be one.

Wanting to be a good communicator is tied to your drive to contribute to a healthy team or family. You are putting effort and attention into how well you talk with, listen to, and support the culture of your team members. If you want to become a great communicator, you should develop a few foundational characteristics:

- ▶ **Curiosity:** Express interest in others and offer more of yourself. Curiosity shows people you care, which creates the space for clearer and more complete exchanges. And the more you know about each other, the more attuned you will be to each other's styles.
- ▶ **Deep listening:** The best communicators we know are also the best listeners. It's not enough to ask questions; you also need to listen to the answers. Listening not only allows us to receive all the information being transmitted but also shows respect for other people—their ideas

and points of view—and encourages openness. Close the laptop, turn off the phone, eliminate distractions, be with the other people fully, and give them your complete attention.

▶ **A sense of humor:** Sharing a laugh not only helps people feel more aligned emotionally but also contributes to the lightness and flow of a conversation. Humor can communicate openness and show that we aren't taking ourselves too seriously. Laughing with people can soothe a tense situation and develop relationships more fully. There is subtlety to humor, of course—all parties in the conversation must find things funny. Welcome humor, but make sure it's not at the expense of your counterparts.

When you reduce unnecessary interpersonal friction, you unlock the true potential of relationships. Curiosity, deep listening, and a sense of humor add up to a sense of presence. When we are fully present in our interactions, it is easier to have a nuanced understanding of, and empathy for, the other people involved. This means you will not only avoid misunderstandings but also will be able to see previously invisible opportunities.

Know Thyself

In high-stakes conversations, a little self-awareness goes a long way. One day Alex was walking into another postdivorce negotiation, and her nerves were uncharacteristically calm. Meeting with the mediator and her ex-husband used to send her into a tailspin of trembling hands and sweaty armpits. She would blank out during detailed conversations about money and often left the meetings feeling disappointed and like she had failed, again, to stand up for herself. But this time she felt calm, collected, and clear.

The difference was that she had learned (by using AIM) how to prepare for high-stakes and highly emotional interactions. In the past, when it mattered most, Alex would show up feeling her worst. She would cower or get defensive, even checking out when contentious points arose. Now, she walked into these meetings feeling clear, centered, and willing to hold her boundaries—mainly because she'd done the work to know herself and approve of that self.

Staying focused, presenting your concerns, showing up fair but strong, and calmly communicating important points has as much to do with what you do before your meeting as what you do during your meeting.

AIM is one way to come into alignment within yourself. It's a valuable exercise and becomes like second nature after you experience how successful you feel in these high-stakes interactions.

The steps involve simply asking yourself to clarify your own intentions (Why are you having this conversation? What do you want to get out of it?), concerns (What issues are you likely to get stuck on? What objections might the other person raise that you can think through in advance? Are there any behaviors to watch out for and plan for?), boundaries (Are there ways of behaving and reacting that you want to avoid this time? If you feel confused or uncertain about something, will you state your desire to have more time to decide? How do you want to engage with the other people or person to protect yourself? Do you need to get an answer to something this time?), and dreams (If this interaction goes perfectly for you, what will happen? What will you get out of it? How will your relationship be after this meeting?).

Going into important or high-stakes conversations brings up emotions, and you might not show up as your best, most confident self without structured preplanning. Writing down your intentions, concerns, boundaries, and dreams and having your notes in front of you for the meeting will lead to much better outcomes.

Emotional Intelligence: The Indispensable Skill
Emotional intelligence is a powerful set of tools in any relationship, whether romantic, parental, or professional. Plainly stated, your emotional (intelligence) quotient (EQ) is your ability to recognize your own emotions and those of others, discern different feelings, and label them appropriately. People with a high EQ are able to use that recognition to guide how they think, speak, and behave. It's about managing and adjusting emotions to adapt to a current situation or conversation to help you achieve your goals.

Emotional intelligence is strengthened as you use AIM. Knowing what EQ entails is the first step to having, growing, and using it regularly as a full-fledged leader and communicator.

Practicing emotional intelligence leads to emotional maturity. Emotionally mature people can handle people, communication, and group dynamics with awareness and fairness by placing equal importance on their own needs and the needs and goals of the group. To have emotional intelligence means you understand your own feelings and motivations and manage them in healthy ways. Emotional maturity is extremely important in today's hyperconnected, hypersocial world.

Your ability to understand and manage your emotions as well as contribute to a safe environment with your emotional maturity is key for success in using AIM, and truly, succeeding at any aspect of business and life.

You might be wondering if you can cultivate, strengthen, and improve these skills. Thankfully, the answer is yes. No matter how high you rate your own emotional intelligence and maturity now, you can always improve them.

Here are ten basics of emotional maturity:

1. **Create space between feeling and acting.** When you're able to notice, observe, and wait a moment between feeling an emotion and reacting to it, you will be more productive. Strong emotional reactions are a result of defensiveness, misunderstanding, or emotional fragility.

It is important to examine and process your emotions, not stuff them down or ignore them. Give yourself permission to pause before responding.

2. **Feel your emotions.** Most of us try to curb our emotions as a way to stay in control. We numb unpleasant emotions with food or alcohol, manipulate our environments, and avoid hard conversations so we never feel vulnerable or uncertain or risk being rejected. Avoiding emotions is usually an effort to stay safe, but when we cut ourselves off from our own hard emotions, we shut down our ability to be aware of other people's emotions and will often miss important contextual information. Give yourself space to feel and be conscious of your emotions.

3. **Develop your compassion.** Compassion for others means having concern for the suffering and misfortune of others. Take your attention off yourself and notice how other people are feeling and what they're experiencing, either verbally, culturally, physically, or emotionally. Compassion for yourself means being able to forgive yourself for mistakes and take care of yourself when things aren't going well.

4. **Admit your fallibility.** Acknowledging your mistakes takes humility and courage and gives others permission to act the same. Although it's easier to get defensive and deny responsibility, sharing when you've made a mistake is a great sign of emotional maturity. Of course, saying

you're wrong must begin with personal awareness. When you are wrong, say so—with grace.

5. **Be aware of your biases.** All humans have biases and prejudices. It's impossible not to—our brains are quite literally wired for bias. It's important to grow and use your awareness of these biases and prejudices and notice how they influence your words, habits, and actions. See where you might be reactively practicing favoritism or prejudice, and explore how you can change these ingrained biases.

6. **Know that you don't know it all.** When we think we know everything, there isn't much room for growth or possibility for teamwork and collaboration. Having expertise in an area doesn't mean that you might not be missing something. Emotionally mature people can admit when they don't know something, be willing to ask questions, and find out a missing piece of information from other experts.

7. **Be flexible.** People with different personalities might respond better when you adjust your style with them. That doesn't mean you give into petty whims or demands or let go of personal boundaries. But meeting people where they are and speaking after listening to them will take you far.

8. **Assume positive intent.** When crises arise, are you quick to blame someone else? In reality, much could be happening of which you're unaware. When things go wrong,

don't immediately rush to blame others or yourself. Get the full picture before making decisions. Identify what you can learn from this situation, realize what you can do differently next time, and create a plan to implement the insight.

9. **Progress over perfection.** People are instinctively afraid to take risks. We prefer to wait until we see exactly how to proceed before we actually start. But perfect plans don't exist! Hold the vision of what you want to achieve, and be willing to find a way to make it happen—mistakes, pivots, lessons, and all. The most successful people and organizations understand that failure is part of growth. If we wait for perfection, we'll die waiting.

10. **Invest in personal growth.** There's an old proverb, either Japanese or Chinese depending on the source, that says: "The best time to plant a tree was twenty years ago. The second-best time is now." Putting time and energy toward your own development pays dividends, no matter when you start. Personal growth work can look like therapy, journaling, energy healing, or personal coaching.

Becoming more emotionally mature and increasing your EQ will help you stay present. In high-stakes interactions, it's common to get caught up in regret about the past or worry about the future. This keeps you stuck and repeating the same patterns. Being fully present is the best way to see opportunities to move forward. Yes, it's important to learn from the past, but reliving mistakes is emotionally draining and pulls down your morale. Learn from it, let it go, and move on.

After you pay attention to growing your emotional intelligence and maturity, you might find it hard to consistently engage with those who aren't developing theirs. This is another point in favor of growing both in yourself: people with a high EQ will notice when you don't have these skills.

Emotionally intelligent and mature people aren't bullies or narcissists—they respect the boundaries of others as well as their own. They aren't jerks, they are not doormats, and they are able to participate in high-stakes, emotionally charged conversations without resorting to manipulation, personal attacks, or defensiveness. In short, they are leaders.

Curiouser and Curiouser

As we mentioned before, one of the most important attributes to bring to any human interaction is curiosity—sprinkled with a touch of confidence. You're connecting with, working with, or making a deal with other people. Being interested in what they want, how they think, and what they're worried about will improve any interaction with them. People like to know that they're important enough to merit your interest!

When you show up as a good listener, asking questions to show you're truly trying to understand someone, that person will feel less of a need to fight to be heard by you.

That person will feel like you're working together, rather than against each other. You would certainly like the same courtesy extended to you.

Some tips on developing curiosity that benefit everyone:

- ▶ **Don't take things for granted.** If you don't understand something clearly, ask questions until you do. Be willing to ask "dumb" questions! You're probably not the only person who isn't clear.
- ▶ **Don't judge someone as boring.** Lean in to listen for the truth of what they're sharing.
- ▶ **See learning as fun.** Having curiosity about someone else makes you much more observant of new ideas and possibilities. When you resolve to be curious, you increase the chances that you'll learn something new.
- ▶ **Read widely and follow your interests.** The joy of discovering new things is like candy for our brains. Make it a habit in your life as well as your work.
- ▶ **Go to an actual library or bookstore.** Browsing the shelves will introduce you to topics and authors you wouldn't specifically search for on a search engine. Coming across a random new idea could open up new worlds!

Adding a dash of confidence to an interaction means feeling into the value of your position and ideas and being willing to stand up for them. When you extend curiosity and empathy to others, they're more likely to extend the same to you.

The Return on Investment of Positive Emotions

You can't have a good team, a strong partnership, or a good conversation without trust. Good relationships exist when people believe they can count on each other, are true to their word, and have the confidence that agreements will be kept.

Trust is also the foundation of psychological safety, the shared belief within a couple or group that it is safe for interpersonal risk taking (more on this in later chapters). With trust, individuals can also feel secure and safe from retribution when they share their personal beliefs and opinions. The most creative and high-performing teams have members who feel accepted, respected, and able to bring themselves forward into the project.

Humans need to believe they are protected from punishment if they fail. Creating a safe place to throw out ideas, good and bad, is a necessity. Otherwise creativity, quirky ideas, and dissenting opinions are less likely.

The broaden-and-build theory from positive psychology shows that positive emotions, including creativity, joy, and engagement, broaden one's awareness and encourage novel, varied, and exploratory thoughts and actions. This broadening also allows us to engage in more divergent thinking, solve complex problems, and cultivate cooperative relationships.

In her work at the University of North Carolina, Barbara Fredrickson found that positive emotions such as trust, curiosity, confidence, and inspiration broaden our minds and help us build psychological and social resources.[2] When we feel safe, we become more open-minded, resilient, motivated, and persistent. Humor and creativity increase.

So how can you improve the emotional landscape of your teams and relationships?

- ▶ **Speak equally.** When all have the same opportunities to speak, without fear of reprisal, then they feel a sense of respect and equality.
- ▶ **Come to conflict as a collaborator.** Humans hate losing even more than we love winning. Bring a sense of "win-win" to your team interactions by asking, How can we all feel like winners here?
- ▶ **Replace criticism with curiosity.** Instead of going on the attack when something goes wrong, get curious about the possible factors. John Gottman's Four Horsemen of the Relationship Apocalypse theory shows how criticism, defensiveness, contempt, and stonewalling lead to breakdown and disengagement. (We avoid these in our marriage, too!)
- ▶ **Ask for feedback.** Show you care about and respect your colleagues by asking them how they received your delivery. It will shine a spotlight on blind spots and model personal awareness and emotional intelligence, which improve people's trust in you. Ask:
  - ▷ What worked in my delivery? What didn't work?
  - ▷ How did it feel to hear what I had to share?
  - ▷ How could I have been more effective in my delivery?

▸ **Finally, ask the big question.** How safe do you feel in this team or this relationship? If in a work context, ask people in your group through a survey how safe they feel and what could foster a stronger sense of safety. How sure do they feel that they won't be punished or called out if they make a mistake?

A growing body of research shows that creating a sense of psychological safety leads to stronger motivation to take on and solve difficult problems, increased engagement, and higher levels of performance. Through a simple, four-step conversational container, we show you how to achieve it all.

THE ALL-IN METHOD (AIM)

AIM is a relationship tool designed to eliminate missing conversations and create a productive emotional context in all of your relationships—professional and personal.

It's a powerful tool that helps break through bottlenecks, speed up productivity, and allow people to show up more authentically.

The method is a simple, four-step, guided conversation that leads you through a transformative exchange. We've used it in a variety of situations, from hiring and sales to project planning and organizational change, as well as for personal conversations about finances, vacations, and even planning our wedding.

AIM is designed to increase clarity and decrease confusion while honoring each person's individuality.

Because it is a structured framework, we find it provides a sense of predictability and safety for emotional conversations. This method makes the personal nature of these conversations feel safer in a work environment.

The simplicity is deceptive. It takes only a short time to learn, but you can spend a lifetime mastering it.

As we looked into why the framework is so powerful and popular with the teams and individuals we taught it to, we noticed that it seemed to reverse engineer something called psychological safety (which we describe in detail in chapter 2).

Although the goals we've outlined above might sound positive and valuable, they are not easy to achieve. It might, in fact, be impossible for a group of people to be fully aligned given their individual values, goals, and desires.

In order to generate alignment, you have to be willing to discover places of misalignment. You even have to be willing to walk away or radically alter your plans based on what you discover.

The alignment you create might be that you mutually agree that the project you're working on is so flawed, or so out of sync with individual goals, that the best course of action is to cancel it altogether.

Radical alignment doesn't mean you do something at any cost; it means you find a course of action that's most aligned with the individuals present. And that might be an agreement to take no action or to end a relationship. This means you need to be both courageous and flexible. From there, great transformation and achievement are possible.

This process requires deep listening and vulnerable sharing. Neither of these happen when you armor yourself against things you don't want to hear or share only the easiest parts of yourself to share.

AIM works best for high-stakes engagements such as starting a team around a critical and complex problem. It also works well in our personal lives when discussing things like money, sex, and child-rearing at home.

When done well, this process helps you discover misalignment early on and provide opportunities for either controlled detonation of interpersonal landmines or, better yet, plans to avoid them or mitigate their impact. This discovery is far better than blindly stumbling onto them.

Although it might result in an early end to whatever is being discussed, we find this a rare outcome, and when it happens, it's far better to have this happen early before too much time, money, or hope has been invested.

More often than not, however, we find that we are aligned and that the process allows us to develop empathy for our counterparts and become their fierce advocates rather than their reluctant companions.

We hope that you'll find AIM as valuable as so many others have and that it will help you find radical alignment with the people around you.

Our Intention for You

The more we know about the people we interact with, the easier it is to understand their perspective and treat them with respect and care. In working and professional relationships, the structure brings fairness to potentially complicated team projects as well as a framework to help various voices contribute in a highly productive manner.

Our intention is that this book and conversation will help bring more empathy, respect, and care into your relationships.

We believe passionately that the world needs more respect and care and are grateful that you've picked up this valuable tool.

we're in this together

"BELONGING IS THE INNATE HUMAN DESIRE TO BE PART OF
SOMETHING LARGER THAN US. BECAUSE THIS YEARNING
IS SO PRIMAL, WE OFTEN TRY TO ACQUIRE IT BY FITTING IN
AND BY SEEKING APPROVAL, WHICH ARE NOT ONLY HOLLOW
SUBSTITUTES FOR BELONGING, BUT OFTEN BARRIERS TO IT.
BECAUSE TRUE BELONGING ONLY HAPPENS WHEN WE PRE-
SENT OUR AUTHENTIC, IMPERFECT SELVES TO THE WORLD,
OUR SENSE OF BELONGING CAN NEVER BE GREATER THAN
OUR LEVEL OF SELF-ACCEPTANCE."
—**BRENÉ BROWN,** *THE GIFTS OF IMPERFECTION*

JILL SOLOWAY, an award-winning writer, director, and pro-
ducer whose credits include *Transparent, Six Feet Under,* and
I Love Dick has a unique way to start a day on the set. They
(Soloway prefers the singular "they" pronoun) gather everyone who is working that day to stand in a circle. At the center
of the circle is a box, and people who want to are invited to
stand on the box and share what is on their minds.

Sometimes people tell personal stories of pain or loss,
sometimes it's how excited they are to work on the day's scene,
or sometimes it's a logistical challenge they face in doing their
job. Anyone can share, no matter their seniority. If people are

working that day, they are welcome to share, whether they are caterers, drivers, extras, crew, or stars like Kevin Bacon.

The result, according to actor Griffin Dunne, is a crew that feels like they are all there to "support each other and that they want each other to do the best work possible that day."

Although this might seem like a costly luxury, actor Katharyn Hahn has a different take. She says that "you feel an investment in everyone making the same thing" and that it is "a valuable time-saving tool and a practical business tool because it gets everybody working towards the same goal."[1]

What they are describing is *aligned action,* and it is the holy grail of teamwork, partnership, and collaboration.

Navy SEALs work toward this outcome as well, albeit in a different way. Their infamous "hell week" is meant to select not only individuals with intellectual grit and physical stamina but also people able to achieve what psychologists call *group flow*—what one SEAL officer describes as "ability to step beyond oneself" so they can merge with the unit and act as one.[2]

SEALs must routinely operate in environments they call volatile, uncertain, complex, and ambiguous (VUCA). In a VUCA context, traditional military practices, such as respect for the chain of command and following the plan, become a liability instead of a strength.

Speed and team agility are the greatest assets in a rapidly shifting environment, and SEALs must achieve a kind of unconscious connection to each other. Often there's no time to ask for permission or to sit down and think things through. The team must flow, and members must be able to sense each other's intentions. When one person is better suited to lead because of their position in the field, the others must follow them. Everyone must think on their feet and be able to both assume and relinquish leadership at a moment's notice.

One SEAL commander says, "More than any other skill, SEALs rely on this merger of consciousness. Being able to flip that switch—that's the real secret to being a SEAL."[3]

The life-and-death environment of guerrilla warfare and the collaborative creativity on a movie set are perhaps extreme cases, but aligned action is no less important in business teams and in family groups.

The "I" in Team

A team is not just a group. It is a collection of individuals who have become something greater. A group doesn't just add but multiplies capabilities. A team is a group of people aligned in their movement and mission to achieve a specific goal and able to complement and amplify each other's talents.

What is a family but a group of people who choose to be aligned for and with each other through life's ups and downs? How will our family thrive as a group if the members don't coordinate and support each other to grow individually?

Teamwork shows up not only at work (e.g., How will our sales team meet the quarterly target if we don't get into aligned action?) or on the field but also at home. We think of our marriage and our family as a team, and we count on each other to encourage, support, and improve ourselves.

Families are teams. This includes biological and chosen families. Each individual member brings unique skills, personality, and energy to the team, just as each sports player has a role and position on a team. A family shares a history and goals, just as a sports team works together to win a game. At times, one player might seem more important than the others. However, one person can't play or win an entire game alone. We need our families to help us live through the happy, good, sad, and painful times. And we need our colleagues to feel more like family if we want to achieve alignment at work.

Families are successful when they act like an aligned team, and so are business teams. And teams of all types can be functional or dysfunctional—and are usually a mixture of both. It is quite common for people to re-create family dynamics in the workplace that come from their families of origin.

In previous eras, when most of the work being done in a community or company was physical labor—either agricultural or industrial—teamwork was less important and team members more interchangeable. This all began to change in the last half of the twentieth century, when work became on average more cognitive. During this era, the market, technology, and demographics began changing at a faster rate. Businesses and even the larger culture are now in a state of near-continuous change, which means we all now live in the

VUCA world, and, as with the Navy SEALs, teamwork has become a core and necessary skill.

Almost all of the highest-paying jobs in recent years require cognitive ability, creative problem-solving, and teammates. Most of the high-value work done today is too complex for a single person to do it all.[4] For instance, when creating software, project managers, engineers, UX designers, analysts, and more must collaborate to create the final product.

These individuals might be highly skilled, but alone they can't finish anything. What they need is a team of other skilled individuals to collaborate with. But the work is complex and often uncertain. For example, the code is often written at the end of a complicated and interconnected process of problem-solving and solution design.

This means they need a team, not just a collection of people. The question of what makes a good team is important in software development, in which the work can be ambiguous and require diverse technical expertise.

What Makes a Team

A few years ago, Google set out to determine what makes a team work well. As a data-driven company, Google decided to be data driven about their quest for great teams and to measure all aspects of this they could. They called the initiative Project Aristotle because of the philosopher's assertion that a whole could be greater than the sum of its parts.[5]

Google had always prioritized hiring high-performing individuals and prided itself on being a meritocracy. Because of its rigorous hiring process, it was always starting with a group of smart and highly skilled individuals. But there were measurable and wide variations in team performance, so Google leaders knew they were leaving value on the table. If they could systematize their approach to creating great teams, the company could be even more successful. Google executives set out to figure out the formula for creating great teams.

Their initial research left more questions than answers—there were few patterns to the data, and many Human Resource Department notions of what creates a great team were wrong or inconclusive. For instance, they found no clear correlation between the performance of the individuals who made up the team and its overall performance—teams of mediocre players (by their standards) could be high performing. Also, teams made up of all introverts, all extroverts, or a mixture of both were as likely to be as great as they were to be mediocre.

The researchers decided the "special sauce" was not in the makeup of the teams, so they turned their attention to team behaviors instead. Did team members socialize outside of work, celebrate birthdays at work, talk a lot or a little, argue or not argue, and so forth? Again, there was no clear pattern in the data telling them how to design or even spot a high-performing team.

Eventually the researchers began to look at subtle behavioral norms, and here Project Aristotle began to pay off. They discovered two characteristics predictive of high-quality team performance.

The first behavior that predicted a high-performing team was equal speaking time among team members. If each person on the team spoke roughly the same amount, the team was likely to be a good one. The team overall could be verbose or quiet, just as long as everyone on the team was speaking around the same amount. But if one or two people spoke more than everyone else, then team performance suffered.

The second characteristic is something they called *average social sensitivity*—if the researchers asked teammates about another teammate's emotional state, would they usually be right in their assessment?

The researchers realized these characteristics indicated that something deeper was happening on the high-performing teams: teammates were paying empathetic attention to each other and interacting respectfully and inclusively.

This led the Google researchers to the work of Harvard professor Amy Edmonson, who has been researching team performance for decades. Edmonson's work identified something called *team psychological safety* as the best predictor of team success.

Team psychological safety is the shared belief among team members that the team is a safe place for interpersonal risk-taking. Edmonson's research has demonstrated a strong correlation between psychological safety and reduced errors on medical teams and increased creativity and problem solving on technology teams.

Two strong indicators of psychological safety are teammates' awareness of each other's emotions and equal speaking time for each team member.

Although there is no research on psychological safety in personal relationships, we find value in applying that lens to our marriage. Being aware of how the other person feels, allowing each other time to speak and share ideas, and prioritizing a relationship in which each partner feels safe to take risks has helped us create a marriage and a life more rewarding and abundant than we have ever experienced before.

In a series of studies, psychologist John Gottman developed a model that predicts a couple's likelihood of divorce with near 90 percent accuracy. Gottman's work hinges on the communication patterns in relationships, and specifically on his Four Horsemen of the Relationship Apocalypse theory:

1. Criticism: This is locating a problem within our partners, not just offering a critique of how their behavior is affecting us. Phrases such as "You never . . .," "You always . . .," and "You are . . . " indicate criticism of them as people instead of critique of their behavior.

2. Contempt: This goes beyond criticism and assumes our moral superiority to our partners. We can communicate it directly ("You think your day was hard? Well, mine

was so terrible you couldn't even handle it!") or indirectly through body language (e.g., rolling our eyes).

3. Defensiveness: We often respond this way to criticism; instead of being curious or taking responsibility for our mistakes, we go on the attack. "I was too busy to do it. Why didn't you just handle it?"

4. Stonewalling: This isn't just asking for a timeout when we feel overwhelmed by a topic, but actively refusing to discuss it. We often respond this way to contempt.

Clinical psychologist David Schnarch has a perspective we find valuable to bring into all of our partnerships, personal and professional. He says, "Love relationships have people-growing processes that call for the best in you to come forward to endure and cope with them. Doing that makes us creative and resilient."[6]

All this adds up to an idea at the center of this book and the All-In Method (AIM): although individual skills and intelligence are essential to team performance, the emotional environment of the team makes all the difference. In other words, teams, like individuals, need both their cognitive intelligence quotient (IQ) and their emotional (intelligence) quotient (EQ) to perform well.

KEEP YOUR CHIN UP

Cognitive science tells us that emotion is essential to cognition. We all intuitively know or have witnessed that emotionally unstable people often make poor decisions. This is because, according to cognitive science, emotions both help us know what to value and affect our nervous system.

If we need to be emotionally stable to make the most of our intelligence as individuals, then it makes sense that teams also need to care for their emotional states *as a collective* to maximize both the group's creativity and speed.

In our marriage and our work, we've learned that *somatic awareness* takes center stage as a necessity to generate both trust and alignment. Somatic awareness is the experience of being in and being aware of our bodies. It's the perception and internal experience of living in our bodies and noticing how we feel physically as we emotionally experience situations and interact with others.

When leading workshops and team offsite meetings, Bob always encourages participants to take care of themselves physically during what can be intense and long days together. He not only encourages "bio breaks"—to eat, go to the bathroom, or get a breath of fresh air—but also shares that he is comfortable with people standing up, stretching, and so on while he is teaching. Tami Simon, founder of Sounds True (publisher of this book), sometimes lies down on the floor during large meetings so she can get in touch with her inner wisdom.

Somatic awareness helps us to feel within ourselves and then reach out to each other and feel the people and space around us. It can inform our ability to assess conditions ("what is happening") more clearly and allow us to act with strategic empathy because we have a better sense of how other people feel.

Through our independent work over the years, including yoga, martial arts, meditation, Alexander Technique, Pilates, and dance, we've been able to connect our individual bodies with our thinking, emotions, vision, and actions. When we feel and know our bodies, we are able to feel and know the people around us; we show up as aligned within ourselves and are therefore more trustworthy.

FEELING INTO TRUST

Trust is a necessary ingredient in creating alignment between people, and AIM is a blue-ribbon, prize-winning recipe for building that trust. When it comes to creating positive and productive relationships, there is perhaps no more important factor than trust. Trust is the essence of leadership; you become a leader by earning the trust of followers, not by achieving a specific rank or position.

Groups are such an essential part of our survival as a species that the instinct to trust is built into our cognition on a deep level.

Anthropologists note that gossip is a pervasive feature of all human groups and might account for the majority of conversation in hunter-gatherer societies. One hypothesis is that groups use gossip to identify who in the group is trustworthy—that is, whose words match their actions and whose don't.

Several studies show that most people, when given the opportunity, will cheat in ways that make them appear more altruistic than they actually are. This is because humans who appear altruistic gain social benefits, but the altruism itself consumes time and resources. So, there is logic to the practice of obtaining benefits without giving up resources (immoral as it might be).

However, gossip and other practices that force transparency and openness allow a community to accurately measure the performance of individuals and decide whom they trust.

However, we are often unconsciously looking for two separate attributes when deciding whom to trust—how competent they are (their skills, strengths, and abilities) and how caring they are (their warmth, companionability, and trustworthiness).

The same studies show that our brains ask the "caring" question first. This makes sense because historically and evolutionarily, trusting someone who is capable but does not care is likely to be a fatal mistake, but trusting someone who cares but is not capable might only be inconvenient because other resources can be found.

This is why psychologists Amy Cuddy, Matthew Kohut, and John Neffinger encourage leaders to connect and demonstrate warmth first before projecting strength. Projecting strength and competence first might actually generate fear instead of trust.

Such insights into how groups operate at their best bring us back to the emotional landscape as the defining feature of a high-performing group. This notion even makes its way into popular culture with heroes such as Buffy the Vampire Slayer, the Avengers, the Fellowship of the Rings, and Harry Potter's crew learning that the dedication they feel for their teammates makes the difference between failure and success. And in case you're wondering, yes, Alex and Bob are both *seriously* into comics, sci-fi, and fantasy.

THE RETURN ON INVESTMENT OF EMOTIONAL INTELLIGENCE AND DIVERSITY

There's a saying that great art comes from friction. Seemingly disparate ideas and elements can be recombined in a unique and powerful way. Alex's Aunt Bo and Uncle Paul have been together for more than forty years and often remark on how they complement each other with different strengths and unique ideas. Respect for each other's creative ideas as artists has led to a beautiful home and decades together as performing musicians.

The same is true in business and the sciences—ideas and innovations that change industries and win awards are often created when disparate worlds collide. James Watson and Francis Crick made history in 1953 when they published a paper describing the structure of deoxyribonucleic acid (DNA). But their work depended heavily on X-ray crystallographic data from the research of Rosalind Franklin and

Maurice Wilkins, who rarely get credit for the discovery because women were not considered worthy scientists at the time. The breakthrough also depended on insights from several disciplines, including those of a Russian composer, which demonstrates that the end result is often a fusion of diverse ideas.

IDEO, the design firm that invented the first mouse for Apple, famously creates diverse teams to ensure creativity. Jimmy Chion, former artist in residence at IDEO, puts it this way: "Because we believe in multi-disciplinary teams, IDEO is diverse. We have psychologists, anthropologists, engineers (of every type), architects, visual designers, interaction designers, writers, and business gurus, to name a few. We also have a food scientist and a surgeon-in-residence because of our work in those industries. We're all united by creating positive impact in the world through design."[7]

Research tells us that teams can be much more creative than individuals, but *how* the team members interact is vital to bringing out this success. The team must be diverse in its skill set *and* its perspective—when people examine the same problem from different angles and bring different skills to developing solutions, then they generate more innovation.

However, the team members must also be able to reconcile all their opposing views. And all team members must feel free to speak up and bring their perspectives forward to avoid groupthink.

Homogenous teams not only tend to have a more limited set of perspectives but also tend to reconcile disagreements more easily or experience fewer of them in the first place. Homogeneity brings shared language and facilitates understanding that allows teams to move more quickly.

Diversity, by definition, increases the possibility of misunderstanding. People from different backgrounds (*identity* or *experience* diversity) and who think differently from each other (*cognitive* diversity) can see the world in disparate ways and might have radically different ideas.

This diversity is a strength, but it is a strength born from friction. The most successful teams are diverse but not derailed by tension. Shane Snow, in *Dream Teams,* puts it this way: "Whenever different ways of thinking collide, they create tension. A cognitively diverse team is like a group of people pulling on different sides of a rubber band. The more tension, the farther the rubber band can launch if it's pointed in the right direction. Psychologists call this cognitive friction—where cognitive diversity collides and creates potential energy."[8]

Teams that fail to learn how to create a positive emotional landscape and a high EQ have more problems embracing their differences and making the most of them. Many teams fail to create inclusive, welcoming environments and revert to homogeneity via attrition—the people who feel different will simply leave when given the chance to work elsewhere.

Another common way teams deal with cognitive friction is to ignore it. Bob, in his work with leadership teams creating organizational change, is usually brought in to reconcile cognitive tension. In fact, it is quite common for new clients to take him aside and tell him he should be aware that they have a uniquely passive-aggressive culture. They say, "We are nice to each other in a way that is not nice," and several have even gone on to say that we call it "[insert name of company] nice," and it's their biggest problem.

As a management coach and consultant, Bob likes to ask client organizations, In the past year, how much of the work you've done has resulted in value delivered to your customer? Answers of less than 25 percent are pretty common—and unsurprising.

When he digs into the problem, he repeatedly finds a culture of burying conflict, in which people agree in a meeting but then ignore that conclusion and go their own way. They say one thing but do another—the very discrepancy gossip is designed to expose. But just knowing that some people are untrustworthy isn't really helpful if you have to collaborate with them to meet your goals. You must find another way.

This "niceness" is the antithesis of collaboration and alignment. When we say radical alignment, we mean that everyone is an enthusiastic yes (a hell, yes) to the project at hand—and to each other. It means we begin with a strong foundation of understanding and trust.

This foundation is something we can return to—deliberately or intuitively—when the inevitable conflicts and misalignments arise. With alignment, these missteps become productive rather than destructive and allow us to quickly return to focus.

To move forward, everyone must be pulling in the same direction. Legendary innovative thinker Geoffrey Moore pointed out in *Dealing with Darwin* that organizations lacking alignment will expend vast amounts of effort but make no progress.

You've probably participated in teams, organizations, or relationships in which other people felt like anchors holding you down, or worse, enemies working against you. However, if other people are both necessary and the problem, what can you do?

Most organizations start by implementing more top-down control. But this practice requires much effort and lowers morale by disempowering the people you most want to motivate. Ordering people around can be incredibly toxic to creative work—that is, all knowledge work.

The company actually needs for people to bring their full selves to the work at hand, but for this to happen, it must find a way to welcome those full selves.

Welcoming in more of the full selves requires developing more empathy for each other. Humans can be messy and unpredictable creatures; without empathy and understanding, it's easy to get frustrated with each other. All of these issues and more require implicit or explicit shared understanding.

▶ "Who will take this task, and when will you get it done?"
▶ "What are our standards of quality?"

> ► "How will we handle vacations and sick days?"
> ► "How do we give feedback to each other?"

There's a reason that one of the habits in Stephen Covey's *The 7 Habits of Highly Effective People* is "Seek First to Understand, Then to Be Understood," and it's not because it feels good. It saves time and energy and makes you a more effective communicator and leader.

One final note: you can generate a more positive emotional landscape even without the other person's knowledge. A former lead Federal Bureau of Investigation (FBI) hostage negotiator, Chris Voss, says developing what he calls *tactical empathy* is the key to saving time in any negotiation. "Tactical empathy is understanding the feelings and mindset of another in the moment and also hearing what is behind those feelings so you increase your influence in all the moments that follow. It's bringing our attention to both the emotional obstacles and the potential pathways to getting an agreement done," says Voss.[9]

In chapter 3, we take a look at the practical steps you can take to begin building an emotional landscape that favors trust, psychological safety, and therefore radical alignment. It starts with something so simple it can be easy to discount—conversation.

the power of conversation

"WHEN YOU SHIFT FROM THAT DOMINANT HIERARCHICAL
THINKING TO A RELATIONAL THINKING, YOU SHIFT FROM
LINEAR THINKING TO ECOLOGICAL THINKING. YOU'RE NOT
ABOVE THE SYSTEM, YOU'RE A HUMBLE SUB-COMPONENT
PART OF THE SYSTEM. YOU LIVE INSIDE OF IT. AND IT'S IN
YOUR INTEREST TO KEEP IT CLEAN AND HEALTHY."
—**TERRY REAL**, *SCENE ON RADIO*, "DOMINATION"

"IN ORDER TO HAVE A CONVERSATION WITH SOMEONE
YOU HAVE TO REVEAL YOURSELF."
—**JAMES BALDWIN**, *NOBODY KNOWS MY NAME*

MANY OF THE SIGNIFICANT moments of our lives start with
a conversation. Deciding to get married, to have children, to
save for retirement, or to start a business are all, ideally, the
result of thoughtful and considered conversations. And not
having an important conversation can often result in negative,
even disastrous, outcomes.

In our work as coaches and consultants, and as partners to
each other, we are often dealing with the effects of missing
conversations that could have prevented a misunderstanding

or dealt with a misalignment or disagreement before it became a critical relationship threat.

The quote that kicks off this chapter mentions *ecological thinking,* and it is worth taking a moment to examine this idea. Ecological thinking means taking a holistic view of the teams you are on and the relationships you are in—and acknowledging that you have a vested interest in keeping them healthy.

A shift from reductive and linear to system-level and holistic thinking means you are less concerned with fairness and more focused on the overall health of the team or relationship and what you can do to make it better. This usually means making sure that all needed conversations are happening—and taking care that *you* show up for them in healthy and constructive ways.

Much of our work is about creating the opportunity and context for conversations. We think of this as the threefold path of alignment:

1. **The right conversation:** Does the conversation focus on the most crucial topic? Are we discussing whether to have children when the real conversation is whether to stay together? At work, are we discussing team composition when, really, we should be discussing project scope and intent? Getting the framework for a conversation right is the first step in a breakthrough.

2. **The right time:** This can be as simple as making sure everyone has time and mental space to have the

conversation—and that they are well rested, not exhausted. Choosing the correct time to have a conversation can make the difference between feeling rushed or feeling spacious and between careful and considered or urgent and fraught. One common piece of relational folk wisdom—never go to sleep angry—can be a formula for staying up all night arguing. Better to get some rest and pick it up in the morning with a bit of distance and perspective.

3. **The right people:** This is often most important at work, where getting the people with actual decision-making power in the room is often a prerequisite for getting things done. At home, it might be that you're discussing moving to a new city but have forgotten to include your children—or worse, your spouse!—in the conversation.

Getting these three elements right can create breakthroughs, and getting them wrong inevitably leads to breakdowns.

In our experience, relationship and organization failures almost always have missing conversations somewhere in the tangled root causes. A common lament among therapists is that couples come to therapy years too late, often many years after they first became aware of the problem. We humans often resist facing our problems, and this avoidance is the source not only of arguments but also of tragedy.

When Roger Boisjoly, an engineer working on the space shuttle *Challenger*, had concerns about the performance of the O-rings, which eventually failed and caused the disaster, he wrote a memo to his superiors—who infamously and disastrously ignored it. The communication (conversation) paths he had available to him did not result in decision makers taking him seriously.[1]

Imagine the difference if Boisjoly had been able to have the right conversation at the right time with the right person —the lives that could have been saved. He did speak up in meetings—but power dynamics and launch urgency prevented his counterparts from heeding, or perhaps even hearing, his concerns.

This event highlights the importance of listening during communication. Conversations are not one-way communication—both speaking and listening are equally important.

Prioritizing conversations means prioritizing listening. Chris Voss, former Federal Bureau of Investigation (FBI) hostage negotiator, says that we need to treat listening as a martial art and that "contrary to popular opinion, listening is not a passive activity. It is the most active thing you can do." Too often we fail to prioritize listening at all and see leadership and negotiation with our loved ones as one-way, charisma-driven games of influence.

Learning to listen can be challenging for many of us. Listening means being open to receiving information that we don't want to hear or that makes us uncomfortable. And developing a norm of listening in groups and organizations is even more challenging. Siloed communication and insistence on going through the proper hierarchical procedures often prevents organizational leaders from listening, even if they personally want to.

You might think that the public failure and loss of life associated with the *Challenger* explosion would be enough for the National Aeronautics and Space Administration (NASA) to make deep changes to how leaders listened and how information flowed in the organization. But in 2003, more than fifteen years afterward, the space shuttle *Columbia* also fell victim to a missing conversation.

This time an engineer named Rodney Rocha was concerned about the launch footage. He thought he saw something come off of the spacecraft during takeoff. The footage of the launch was low resolution, and it was hard to be certain, but Rocha watched the footage repeatedly and became increasingly concerned that the space shuttle had been damaged.

Following standard protocol, he wrote emails alerting his superior to his concerns. But the information never reached the right leaders, or if it did, they did not act. It was later confirmed that he saw a piece of insulating foam come loose and make a large hole in the leading edge of the wing. During reentry, this hole caused the shuttle to crash.

In one large meeting with a senior project manager, Rocha had had the chance to speak up. When asked by a reporter why he hadn't used the opportunity, Rocha said, "I just couldn't, I'm too low down."[2] The nature of power, his position, and social norms at NASA caused him to second-guess himself, leading to a tragic outcome.

Real leadership takes courage. When we take the lead in a work project or in addressing an important challenge at home, we must be able to hear criticism of our point of view even if we don't want to hear it—which, for most of us, is always.

We also need to remember that most people don't want to rock the boat. It is uncomfortable for most of us to disagree with our peers and especially difficult to disagree with our superiors. Even in our marriages or family systems, upsetting the natural order of things feels dangerous.

Statistics have shown that one reason brainstorming is of limited value is that people often pick up on subtle social cues about what the leader wants and then simply confirm it. This can be subconscious or conscious—disagreeing with the boss can often be a career-limiting move.

This means one of the primary jobs of any team leader, parent, or spouse is to create a context in which it is safe for people to tell you difficult news. We must invite people into conversations and do what it takes for them to be honest. Otherwise you will hear only things that confirm your biases and decisions. The people around you will feel unenthusiastic at best or even actively resentful at worst.

Conversations about subjects that engage both our intellect and our emotions—in other words all important topics—are difficult to have.

In chapter 2, we talked about the passive-aggressive orga-nizational cultures Bob encounters in his work. In these cultures, having difficult conversations has become almost impossible. Sometimes the conversation that needs to happen is "You're fired" or "I quit" because the people and the project or organization are a bad match. But more often than not, the missing conversation is one in which opposing viewpoints are expressed and eventually reconciled.

The ability to welcome and integrate diverse perspectives and skills is at the core of healthy collaboration and creativity—and therefore of innovation. Being part of a great team means cocreating an environment in which people feel free to share ideas that run counter to what the group expects—bad news or countercultural ideas—and in which the group is able to reconcile opposing viewpoints and move forward. They don't get stuck in analysis and a never-ending search for consensus or fall apart because of conflict.

Amy Edmonson, the Harvard researcher who coined the term *team psychological safety*, notes that it doesn't take much to curtail communication when a power dynamic is present. Nurses, for instance, often reflexively defer to a doctor's authority and fail to speak up, even when a potentially life-threatening mistake is made.

During her research, Edmonson interviewed a nurse named Christina who had noticed that a doctor failed to prescribe a potentially life-saving medicine to a premature baby. "In hesitating and then choosing not to speak up, Christina was making a quick, not entirely conscious, risk calculation. . . . She told herself the doctor knew better than she did, and she was not confident he would welcome her input."[3]

Although it is easy to put the onus on Christina and say she should have more backbone, the truth is that we are busy at work doing the same job day after day, and we are tired. It is not realistic just to depend on individuals to do better. We must also create a context and culture in which conversation and even conflict are welcomed and encouraged.

Too often it is easier to just let something slide than it is to create a potential conflict. This is amplified if the person we disagree with is of higher status and/or is prone to taking offense and making things difficult for us.

Leaders must create an environment in which disagreement is welcome. They do this by listening and creating opportunities for people to be willing or even expected to speak up.

As Edmonson says, "Psychological safety is not a personality difference but rather a feature of the workplace that leaders can and must help create."

Creating this kind of workplace can be challenging. We are all busy and get stressed at times. Just working on our individual emotional response isn't enough. We also must consciously create the opportunity for people to share.

These opportunities can be subtle. As a facilitator, when Bob wants people to share, he is careful to ask, What questions do you have? He will then be silent and wait for someone to speak. If he wants to move on, he asks, Any questions? Then he introduces the next item quickly with little break. This is surprisingly effective.

Power dynamics are, of course, present not only at work but also in our personal lives. Humans are hardwired to fit in, for the most part. David Schnarch, a clinical psychologist specializing in relationships, points out that most couples experience a differential in desire (e.g., for sex, date nights, or a tidy home), and the low-desire partner has all the power. This is because if the high-desire partner forces the low-desire partner to act, it will be based on manipulation, or worse, physical assault.

Schnarch goes on to say that the solution lies in the people who find themselves in control being willing to listen, learn, and stretch. Although power differentials are perhaps inevitable, they can shift day to day and topic to topic, so it is in all parties' interest to be vigilant about inclusivity and fairness.

It often doesn't take much to change how people interact, but you must be deliberate about it.

RULES OF THE CONVERSATIONAL ROAD

The All-In Method (AIM) is a structured conversation designed to create space for the most common missing parts of collaborations and exchanges. It has a clear beginning and end, and it invites people to be honest and vulnerable with each other. We believe that having rules for important, high-stakes, or emotional conversations sparks creativity and inclusivity and offers a higher likelihood of success.

When you are in a position of leadership, one of the best ways to welcome input is a facilitated agenda. Bob's standard practice for facilitating meetings is to start off with a personal question: What has your attention? What are you looking forward to? Just asking the question creates an environment in which people will share something important to them and will allow others to develop empathy or at least awareness of how others are feeling. This, remember, is an essential component of psychological safety.

We recommend trying this in all your meetings. It is similar to Jill Soloway's box practice but perhaps easier to adopt in more traditional business environments.

This pairing of a clear, step-by-step (dare we say *masculine*) structure with an invitation to be vulnerable, emotional, and personal (dare we say *feminine*) in what we communicate creates the opportunity many leaders seek. It creates a sense of safety that can unlock deep emotions and real vulnerability.

It works in the same way a roller coaster allows us to safely experience the feeling of imminent death. Think of a structured conversation as a kind of emotional amusement park that allows you to experience the thrill with more control and less danger.

Bob once led an AIM conversation with a deeply divided leadership team. A few key members were on the verge of quitting—the organization was unstable and siloed, and people were fearful of each other. The first round of the conversation was about *intentions* (e.g., why they wanted to be part of this organization and to have it succeed). One leader told a deeply vulnerable story of childhood neglect, connected to his personal sense of purpose for the organization, that brought people in the room to tears.

Bob was stunned; he had not expected this level of vulnerability. After the session the whole tenor of the room had changed. It had gone from a feeling of defensiveness to one of mutual respect and care. Although the rifts were never fully healed in that organization, this session set up a context in which people in high-stakes conversations more easily found common ground.

Priya Parker designs high-stakes conversations for a living. She has done conflict-resolution work in some of the most sensitive environments imaginable. Parker emphasizes what she calls *rules-based gatherings*. These are events at which the host is explicit about the expected behavior from participants.

A Jeffersonian dinner is a long-running example of a rules-based gathering. These are designed based on dinners Thomas Jefferson used to host. The dinners are limited to fourteen people and are driven by one rule—you are not allowed to talk to the person next to you but must speak to the table as a whole. This creates a specific kind of interaction and dialogue.

Parker says, "Rules-based gatherings, controlling as they might seem, are actually bringing new freedom and openness to our gatherings."[4] They do this by allowing us to relax because we know exactly what is expected of us. Parker contrasts this with etiquette—unspoken implicit rules that come out of a specific culture and class.

Rules-based gatherings are more welcoming and inclusive for people from a variety of backgrounds because they spell out the rules of engagement and don't require extensive study or create potential embarrassment for newcomers.

Rules-based gatherings are at the heart of many modern ways of working that have appeared in the previous few decades. One example is agile software development that makes use of what are sometimes called *ceremonies*—specialized meetings with set agendas and explicit expected behaviors that happen on a cadence.

One example of an agile ceremony is a daily standup meeting in which the members of a small development team meet for fifteen minutes, usually standing around their task board, and each person in turn updates the others on what they worked on yesterday, what they intend to work on today, and where they are blocked or need help. This simple ritual prevents problems before they arise, promotes transparency, and creates a feeling that members are on a team and supported rather than an isolated cog in a machine.

In our homes and relationships, rules and rituals can become new family traditions. In her award-winning documentary *ScreenAgers,* physician Delaney Ruston shows the impact of technology and screens on the well-being of teens and their families. She created "tech talk Tuesdays" as a way for families to have ongoing conversations about how they use technology (both positive and potentially negative), reviewing the house rules for technology use, and opening conversation between all members of the household. This weekly check-in allows parents to feel up to date on how everyone is using their gadgets and helps kids feel they have both boundaries and some autonomy in how they're using technology.

One of our favorite family rituals is to eat dinner together and play a game called "High, Low, Hero." People share their high and low points from the day as well as a moment in which they helped someone. This leads to much richer and more rewarding interactions than questions such as, How was your day?, which often result in one-word answers. It also allows for an honest conversation in which our son gets to see that adults have complex lives. Much like leaders who make personal, vulnerable authenticity a priority to help their teams feel safe, parents can bring those same attributes to their homes.

Reengineering Conversations

Creating a new kind of conversation in your relationships at work or at home is a great place to start shifting a relationship dynamic. Getting the right topic, people, and time are the basics, but there is a deeper element.

As we've said, a conversation is not just a one-way sharing of information but an exchange. For conversations to be successful, we must not only receive what is being communicated but also be willing to be changed by it. One or more parties in a conversation must shift if the situation is going to change, and change is the whole reason we are having conversations in the first place.

In chapter 4, we will introduce you to AIM.

4

set the stage

THE POWER OF the All-In Method (AIM) lies in its structure and intentionality. It might feel strange, even forced, at first, but if you want different results you need to have conversations differently. Hope is not a strategy. And over time, AIM will get easier and more natural.

Most people, most of the time, don't structure their conversations. But there is real power to having a method—as the saying goes, "If you don't know where you're going, you'll end up somewhere else." This doesn't mean we want you to forgo surprise and conversational serendipity. We are saying that there is great power in being intentional and creating a shared context for *why* you are having an interaction. And that preparation is key.

AIM is a simple, guided conversation that helps two or more people gain clarity and develop a deeper understanding of, and appreciation for, each other and their shared experience.

The method is useful whenever you are engaging in conversations that feel important and are likely to raise deep emotions—and let's be honest, that's 95 percent of human conversations.

Ideally, you want to have this conversation before emotions are high or the project gets too complicated, but it can also work if you want to hit the "pause" button on a project that's going in a bad direction and reset its trajectory.

AIM is designed to raise, reveal, and share previously unspoken assumptions, expectations, fears, and desires, which so often lead to conflict. It also creates a framework in which there is a high degree of psychological safety for us to say things we might find difficult to articulate.

As much as we try to ignore it, business and family life are complicated by the fact that humans are emotional creatures and regularly act illogically. AIM works because it addresses our innate emotionality and brings to the surface hidden assumptions and pieces of information—even ones we hide from ourselves.

If we know where the emotional landmines are buried, we can avoid them or, even better, have a kind of controlled detonation. This knowledge means we won't stumble upon them accidentally, which often creates a chain reaction of conflict and disappointment.

PREPARING PARTICIPANTS

Winston Churchill once said, "I'm always willing to learn, but I'm not always willing to be taught." This reflects a common human dynamic in which we might be open to change and growth but want it on our terms. So, although you might be coming to a conversation after reading this book with a lot of excitement and energy for the topic, the other people you want to talk with might not be as ready or as enthusiastic. The conversation will go much better the more prepared they are.

One obvious way to prepare them would be to send them a copy of this book with a note explaining why you want to talk to them. For example, you could say, "I'd love to use this method to discuss our financial future so we both can get what we want." At the very least, we recommend a brief introduction to the method either by sharing the cheat sheet in the appendix (also available on our website in shareable, printable form) with your partner, friend, or team well in advance or setting aside time before the conversation so that people can wrap their heads around the format. Some people are resistant when new ways of thinking are sprung on them!

One of Alex's clients printed out the cheat sheet and gave it to her spouse on a Friday evening, requesting child-free time on Saturday afternoon for this conversation. She knew her husband would appreciate and need time to think up responses and ideas before sitting down to talk.

In Bob's corporate consulting, he presents this conversation as a project-focused meeting, introducing the format at the beginning and leading the team through the steps as the facilitator. We provide more thoughts and advice on acting as a facilitator later in the book.

Think about the person or group of people you want to have this conversation with. Honor the time they might need to prepare and process. Most people aren't used to being led through a structured conversation, so it might feel strange at first. Are they the kind of people who need a day or two to think about how they'll talk and share? Would they like to have a copy of the structure in advance? Or are they able to go with the flow while you take the lead and guide the conversation? Providing materials in advance is especially helpful when people are cautious or need to feel in control.

If you're having the conversation with children, we recommend framing the steps with a vocabulary that matches their maturity. For example, maybe your five-year-old doesn't understand boundaries, but you can ask them what they don't want in relation to your topic. For instance, when our son was very young, we decided we wouldn't make him hug any strangers or even family members when he didn't want to. We told him we would let him decide who to hug, and this was a boundary for him.

SETTING THE STAGE

Up to now, we've been helping you to set the stage to begin using this method—your mindset and the physical environment are equally important. When you use AIM, it's important to be present. Set aside time and create a space where you won't be interrupted or distracted. Put cell phones out of sight, reserve a conference room, put the kids to bed, get out of the house, or go to a secluded place—a setting in nature is wonderful for it.

With business teams, we use AIM in either a stand-alone formal meeting or as part of a longer session. When we use it for personal issues as a couple, we love to have the conversation over dinner (without alcohol), on a walk or long drive, or on the couch with tea late at night.

The conversation doesn't have to take a lot of time, but it must have a feeling of thoroughness. We've run through the four steps in five minutes about simple family outings, and we've taken hours to dive into our quarterly business goals. Your first thoughts will usually be less informative and valuable than the ones that come later.

Take your time, be curious, and allow for some pauses while the speaker gets clearer. This process can feel uncomfortable, but on the other side of discomfort is where the good stuff usually is.

You'll want to limit the focus of the conversation to something specific such as a project launch or the next fiscal quarter. Within a relationship conversation, you can focus on a single issue such as budgeting, sex, or children.

The important thing is to be clear about what you're discussing and to ensure that everyone treats the topic with respect. It helps if each person finds the topic vital, but sometimes it will be more important to one person than it is to another. That's okay as long as the person who finds it less important still takes the conversation seriously.

Remember, one of the values here is developing what Chris Voss calls *tactical empathy*. This is not just about feeling good or being nice; it's about stepping into other people's shoes for a moment so you can see the world from their perspective.

Knowing, and having sensitivity to, what someone else wants is one of the surest ways to get what you want. In the majority of conversations, most of us are waiting for our turn to speak and only half listen. Do your best to truly hear the other people in this conversation.

Although listening to others can be challenging, it can also be difficult to share your own feelings with vulnerability. So, have compassion for each other, whether speaking or listening. The process gets easier with each conversation, and the structure brings security, helping you feel safe to reveal more about your inner workings each time.

Roles

There are two roles for the conversation—speaker and listener; each participant plays each role, switching back and forth as you progress through each of the four parts.

The Speaker

When speaking about something important, you might find it hard to express yourself in clear, complete thoughts.

Many people become clearer as they speak—whereas others might become less clear.

Because there is a format to these conversations, and because there is an intention set at the beginning that shines a light on safety and listening, many people are able to "find their words" using this process when previous attempts have failed.

If the topic is particularly sensitive, having participants silently write their answers to themselves before sharing can be powerful.

Be brave. Be compassionate. Be patient.

Challenge yourself to be complete. The conversation is most successful when there's a slight feeling of danger.

"Should I be saying this?"

"Is this too much?"

"Am I being too revealing?"

All of these are reasonable responses to vulnerability—and also signs that you're probably getting somewhere good. Vulnerable communication almost always feels a bit scary.

Not all things should be shared in all environments, so use your best judgment on how much to share. That said, we find that erring on the side of sharing too much is where you get the real value out of this conversation.

If you run out of things to say, that's all right, but don't end your turn prematurely. It can be incredibly valuable to sit with the discomfort of not knowing what to say and ask yourself, What else is there?

The Listener
If the speaker is going to be vulnerable, thorough, and honest, then we need to listen in a way that creates a feeling of safety. Being curious is a good start.

It's up to the listener to be genuinely curious. You can ask questions—especially open-ended ones such as, Can you tell me more about that? You can also ask, Is there anything else you want to share about that? Be careful not to use a question format to express a judgment—for example, Are you sure that's a good idea? Don't you think something else would be a better idea?

If you're feeling triggered or excited, it's often best just to say nothing. Jumping in with your thoughts can indicate that you have a vested interest in what other people mean by what they say. Your job as the listener is to receive, not to guide, call out, or generate insights for the speaker.

Be especially suspicious of an urge to call out someone on their BS, as is common in personal development circles. This is more often about your own projections than it is about the other person. It will leave the speaker feeling less safe and you less curious. And remember that even nonverbal cues—such as an eye roll—can communicate disapproval or even contempt and have a chilling effect on the speaker's willingness to share.

Speakers, of course, might be full of BS—aren't we all sometimes?—but it's so much more valuable for them to discover this fact for themselves than it is to have someone point it out.

If you find yourself expressing judgment or anger, that's okay. We all mess up. Just be prepared to forgive yourself and each other and do what's necessary to go back to the conversation.

The goal is to reach a deeper understanding of each other's perspectives even, and especially, on difficult topics. And these are often a bit fuzzy and even contradictory. That's fine.

Humans are, at least in part, illogical by nature, so expecting someone (even yourself) to be completely logical and clear at all times is an unreasonable and illogical stance in itself.

Respect, curiosity, and gentleness are your goals. Listen, ask questions if you need help understanding what the speaker means, and keep the focus on understanding, not judging, their communication.

In the workplace, it might feel uncomfortable and even dangerous to open the door to emotionality. We don't want to pressure people into vulnerability. If you're a leader bringing this method to a team, it's important to consider your team's ability to handle the conversation with care and mutual respect. It will be up to you to set the tone—your team will likely be only as vulnerable as you are.

That said, most workplaces will benefit greatly from more engagement and motivation on the part of their teams. In most cases, this engagement requires people to feel personally invested in the work and the team, and there is no better way to generate that connection than through empathy, trust, and shared intentions.

AIM is designed to create a safe environment in which to have high-stakes, personal conversations. It's also self-paced, meaning people can share as deeply, or as close to the surface, as they feel ready to. If you are a leader, it's often best for you to go first and set the example of vulnerability and honesty, which can feel like a breath of fresh air in many work environments.

We've had the conversation with teams ranging from high-ranking executives at major corporations to product teams at startups, and the result has always been improved teamwork and performance.

For this conversation (any meeting, really), it can be useful to establish a single facilitator. Their job is to keep the conversation moving along and to prevent crosstalk while someone is sharing.

If we are self-facilitating, it can be too tempting to go down a conversational rabbit hole and begin to debate or problem solve. This conversation is for sharing, not working, and having a facilitator will help you keep on track.

You can select a facilitator from the group who will also be a participant. If you go this route, we strongly recommend that this *not* be the highest-paid person or the most powerful or verbose person in order to keep power dynamics in check and encourage more open sharing.

You can also bring in a skilled facilitator external to the team. This usually creates the richest and most valuable conversation, and we highly recommend it if possible. Check gettingtohellyes.com to learn more about facilitation.

Information, Not Orders

One final note on listening and speaking: in order to listen with curiosity and speak with vulnerability, it's helpful to remember that we are sharing and hearing information, not taking or giving orders.

When I share my dreams or fears with my partner, I'm not requiring that they do anything with the information. I'm just letting them know who I am and how I feel.

Just because our teammates want something doesn't mean we have to give it to them, and just because we share that we want something doesn't mean we'll get it. We often want others' feelings to be almost identical to our own. But appreciating difference can be as important as seeing similarity for generating radical alignment.

We aren't ordering "off the menu" when we speak or taking orders when we listen. We are just learning about each other (and often ourselves, too) and developing more empathy and understanding.

Speak with courage and vulnerability, listen with gentleness and compassion, and 99 percent of the time a conflict will be resolved naturally.

CHAPTER SUMMARY

▸ Be deliberate about the intention and structure of the conversation as a way of helping it go well.

▸ Prepare participants by giving them this book and/or the cheat sheet in the appendix in advance so they know what's coming.

▸ Pick a distraction-free space and set aside time to have the conversation.

▸ Be clear about the topic you'll be discussing and why it is important to the participants.

▸ Speakers should be as honest and vulnerable as they are able given the circumstances.

▸ It is the listener's job to encourage sharing, and this is best done by being nonjudgmental and curious and not negatively reacting either verbally or with body language to what the speaker shares.

▸ The goal of the conversation is to create a full and complete understanding of each other—this does not mean you agree with all that is said, only that you truly hear it.

▸ Speak with courage and vulnerability and listen with curiosity and without judgment to create the richest interactions.

have the conversation

Now that the stage is set and roles are understood, you're ready to have the conversation. We recommend having it in the order presented because it creates the richest exchange and tends to end on a high note.

Remember: listen with compassion and curiosity, and speak with courage and vulnerability.

The conversation is broken into four parts. Take them one at a time, with each participant taking turns as speaker and listener before moving on to the next part. It's fair to ask clarifying questions between parts, but we like to keep crosstalk to a minimum. This process keeps the emotional arc of the conversation consistent across the room and, in our experience, generates the best outcome.

Clarify the Topic

The first thing you need to do is clarify what you'll be discussing. Sometimes doing so is easy, but sometimes it can present a challenge.

Sample topics:

- ► Business
- ► Team/project launch or relaunch
- ► Plan for next quarter or year
- ► Marketing (or other) event plan
- ► Sales meeting preparation
- ► New product plan
- ► Governance changes/additions
- ► Hiring and onboarding new people
- ► Personal
- ► Moving
- ► Vacation or party plan
- ► Finances
- ► Sex
- ► Child-rearing
- ► Housework
- ► Parent-child dynamics
- ► Retirement
- ► College

Next, name why you want to talk about this topic. A good setup would be something like:

- ► Incentive compensation policy—so we make sure it encourages the right behavior
- ► Project X—so we can be a great team
- ► Conference plan—so we include all the important topics and hire the right services

- ▶ Family summer vacation—so we all have fun
- ▶ Your children's college degrees—so they get degrees that serve them best and we are fully supportive of them

If each participant takes responsibility for being personally clear on what is being discussed and why, then the setup will go smoothly.

When two people are using this process for a personal conversation, one person will likely feel more strongly than the other about the need for the conversation. If this is the case, the person with less motivation should do what they can to take on the conversation with as much interest as if it were their own idea. Not only does it make for the best communication but also you'll certainly be on the other side with another topic and will appreciate your partner's effort in taking this approach with you—today, we talk about finances (important to you), and tomorrow, we talk about house cleaning (important to me).

Now you are ready to have the conversation.

Take each section one at a time, giving each person the chance to be both speaker and listener before moving on to the next section.

Intentions

In this first section we discuss our intentions for the topic at hand. This is the overarching *why,* and it will likely be different for each person involved. Bringing these broad or fundamental differences to the surface early is helpful in avoiding or understanding disagreements in the details later. Differences are 100 percent welcome and can often be accommodated with thoughtful cooperation. In many cases they even enrich the experience. But if you aren't aware of differences up front, they can lead to a lot of trouble down the road.

Too often we humans think our experience is universal, and others are doing things for the same reasons we are doing them. For example, when a couple goes on vacation, one partner could want to get some much-needed rest, and the other is looking for adventure and an escape from monotony. These need not be mutually exclusive goals, but if the couple starts talking about the trip itinerary first, things might quickly devolve.

One thing to note is that intentions are not our dreamed-of outcomes or best-case scenarios; those get discussed later in the conversation. Although we might dream that a work project will be so successful it will make us millions of dollars, our intention is more mundane: we are doing a project to make money, learn something new, and enhance our reputation. Intentions, therefore, tend to be concise and to the point.

Before we began using this conversation in our marriage, Alex all too often felt overwhelmed at the beginning of "important chats." This one simple step helped her to calm her energy and quiet her mind. For Alex this was a game-changer because it forced her to get clear on what she wanted—often the first step to getting it.

Being clear about our intentions can alter the way we approach an action. Knowing our values and goals can generate flexibility and creativity in aligning with a partner, a client, or your team in a way that meshes with those values.

Also, sharing our intentions has a way of creating allies. When we know why people are doing something, we can help them achieve that goal. It can also help generate trust, which is often more about predicting someone's behavior than about what that behavior is. Understanding their motivations helps make people's behavior more predictable.

Although answers might be short, the speaker will still want to offer some color and help the listeners connect to their values and their larger life goals. That's where intentions really come alive. For example, when Bob works on projects, he frequently brings in collaborators and loves to know what they want out of the project. Money tends to be an obvious, tangible outcome everyone is after, but often there are intangibles such as learning new things, building a reputation, gathering information for a writing project, and so forth. When Bob is aware of these other goals up front, he notices opportunities to allocate people in different ways on projects.

Prompt questions for this section are highly dependent on the topic under discussion. You can focus either on the personal *why* of each participant and/or more broadly address the *intentions* of the team. The example prompts below are good starting places, but feel free to craft your own.

The idea is to get clarity and alignment on the overarching reason the topic is important and get participants thinking in a positive, problem-solving way.

Prompts:

- ► Why do you want to
    - ▷ be a part of this project?
    - ▷ go on this vacation?
    - ▷ save and invest our money?
    - ▷ start this business?
    - ▷ improve our sex life?

- ► Why are we
    - ▷ making changes to our organization?
    - ▷ launching this product?
    - ▷ scheduling this all-hands meeting?
    - ▷ getting married?
    - ▷ having children?
    - ▷ moving to Denver?

- ► What do you value when it comes to this topic?

- ► What are your personal goals when it comes to this topic?

Remember, this section is not about what you hope or dream will happen—those come later in the conversation. Answers to intention questions will therefore be short and to the point, such as:

- ▶ Make money
- ▶ Have fun
- ▶ Learn something new

Intentions are easy to articulate if you're already clear about what you want to achieve or solve. If you find yourself with no answer, or a vague one, it's a good opportunity to get clear and more precise.

We often do things out of fear, habit, or obligation. For example, we might be launching a project because our boss told us to. If the *why* you articulate is external or based on a feeling of "having to," this is a good opportunity to interrogate your reasons a bit more deeply and perhaps question these motivations.

You might find that, yes, because of your boss's personality, you are doing the project out of fear of getting fired, but going one layer deeper you discover that you believe the project is a good idea for the company. You might, of course, also discover it is not. You might also find that your original feeling of obligation is actually connected to a deeper desire, such as supporting teammates or being a valued team member.

Because Bob works project to project, he gets the chance to ask himself this question often. This has given him the opportunity to create a small checklist he goes through as he examines a project and debates taking it or not. Not every project needs to check all the boxes, but reviewing his intentions helps him be, well, intentional about the work he takes on and, therefore, creates better outcomes for his clients and his projects.

His intentions are in two blocks: outcomes and compensation.

Outcomes:
- ▸ Better collaboration (between humans doing good in the world)
- ▸ Increased power for marginalized people
- ▸ Increased ecological sustainability (near or long term)

Compensation:
- ▸ Make money now
- ▸ Grow my reputation
- ▸ Grow my reach
- ▸ Be with people I enjoy, love, and respect

As you speak, it can be helpful to call out experiences that feel uncomfortable. This part of the conversation is about personal motivations, which are likely to feel a bit selfish at times. A little bit of discomfort in the spirit of authenticity is okay and even encouraged. For example, when using this conversation in setting up a new consulting project team, Bob always says one of his intentions is to make money—along with learning new things and delighting the customer. Talking about money violates a common taboo, so this unexpected statement can encourage more openness and vulnerability—the building blocks of trust and alignment.

Concerns

This part of the conversation is about getting all your concerns out on the table. In many ways the human brain is primarily a worry machine. We look for problems and focus on what could go wrong. This makes sense from an evolutionary perspective because for most of human history one wrong move could be the difference between life and death.

Srinivasan Pillay, author, psychiatrist, and brain researcher, tells us that the amygdala is calmed when we speak concerns out loud. The amygdala is at the center of the limbic system—one of the oldest parts of our brains—and is the source of much of our emotional life, including anxiety and fear. Sharing your concerns can help you to notice where you might be triggered, release tension, and even let go of a false story.

When we are asked to articulate our concerns, it forces us to become conscious of them. This can transform anxiety, which tends to be generalized, into fears, which are more specific. What is interesting about the process, and we've seen this play out time and again in a variety of contexts, is that when we become specific about a fear, it either evaporates or it becomes easier to address.

As we considered taking on this book project together, we both were aware that it brought up anxiety. We have both previously had bad experiences in both personal and professional relationships and had been cautious about jeopardizing our marriage with a potentially stressful project—like writing a book!

When we went through the conversation about it, we were forced to articulate our specific concerns, which, for both of us, boiled down to a fear that the stress of publishing would cause us to break up. After we articulated this clearly, two things happened. First, we laughed. We have taken great care to create a strong partnership, and the idea that we would let stress spiral out of control until it broke us up actually seemed ridiculous.

Second, we were able to articulate an agreement—a kind of boundary, discussed in the next section—that either of us could unilaterally call a pause to the project if we felt it was negatively affecting our experience of the relationship.

Prompt questions for this section are relatively easy to articulate because getting most people to talk about their concerns is pretty easy. If what you're doing is important, then you're going to have some concerns. This is your chance to do some worst-case-scenario planning and worry as much as you like. Often, your worries aren't clear but exist as just a vague sense of dread or fear. During this section, you want to try to name these fears and be as specific as possible.

Here are a few prompt ideas to get you started:

- ▶ What worries you about the team, our plan, and so on?
- ▶ Where do you think we will run into trouble?
- ▶ What about the way we are approaching this might keep you from getting what you want out of it?
- ▶ Let's say it's two years from now and this has gone horribly—why do you think it did?

Often, just articulating a concern is enough to banish it, so let yourself and others speak until all of it comes to the surface. As the speaker, be sure to bring up concerns that involve possible effects on the listeners—this is valuable information and demonstrates empathy and care, so don't be stingy with it.

Concerns can be related to psychological outcomes and feelings or might have real-world impact. Here are some common themes we hear from ourselves and others when participating in this process:

- ▶ I might get angry.
- ▶ You might feel bad, which would upset me.
- ▶ We might argue or disagree.
- ▶ I might have to face a personal fear such as that of public speaking.
- ▶ You might think I'm a jerk.
- ▶ I might not know what to do or how to do it.
- ▶ I might regret choosing this over something else.
- ▶ Concerns can also relate to real-world outcomes such as:
  - ▷ We might deplete our budget with no return on investment.
  - ▷ We might lose customers.
  - ▷ We might lose money.
- ▶ I might not be able to give this enough focus, given my other commitments.
- ▶ I might have to stay up all night and miss sleep and family time.

Notice that concerns might bring up values and assumptions. In some cases, they might even help you refine your intentions. Although this process is linear, it's fine to revisit previous sections if something becomes clearer. The whole point of the process is to create more clarity and gather full information, so don't hesitate to go a step or two back if you realize something.

Often during this section, easy fixes for a concern emerge—agreements, rules, budgetary triggers, and so forth—that could mitigate or eliminate the concern. This is wonderful, but for now keep it to yourself, perhaps by jotting down a quick note. The All-In Method (AIM) is not for problem solving but for information sharing, and suggesting an agreement or rule can derail the process. It's best to create agreements and plans after the full process is complete.

Boundaries
Boundaries are your personal non-negotiables. They are a line that you won't cross yourself, or a line that others aren't welcome to cross.

Boundaries stem from rules individuals have in place—often around self-care, family, and community commitments. They work best when they are firm rather than vague and flexible. Ideally, you have strong boundaries in both personal relationships and at work. But honestly, this is an area in which many of us need a bit of help and permission to be clear.

For instance, we don't often have conversations about personal boundaries in professional contexts because often the assumption is that work comes before everything else. But if we don't encourage good personal boundaries at work, we are creating an environment that isn't conducive to creativity or productivity. If we want people to do their best work, we must encourage them to be at their best when on the job. And being at their best means being well rested, well fed, and free of distractions—in other words, engaging in self-care.

We all have competing commitments—family, community, and projects at work. Letting the listener know up front about our commitments outside of the topic at hand is important. It helps us become allies for each other and collectively create a team environment that helps us be fully present as individuals.

You can think of boundaries as design criteria for a shared experience. Designers will tell you that constraints are needed to generate creativity and that no good design happens without them. As you discuss each team member's personal boundaries, you articulate what the team needs to be at its best.

It is kind to share your boundaries with others because inadvertently violating a boundary can create stress, destroy trust, and even irrevocably harm relationships.

A useful concept in articulating boundaries comes from the psychology of habit change—it's called a *bright line*. Bright lines are easy-to-understand binary rules, meaning there is no ambiguity or gray area—you are either on one side of the line or the other, and there is no in-between state. They are valuable in establishing good habits because we know when we are following them and when we aren't. So, we don't have to think too much about whether we are on track.

For instance, if we are trying to eat better, bright lines such as "Eat green vegetables at every meal" and "Eat no processed sugar" take less brain power and willpower to monitor than vague rules such as "Try to eat less" or "Don't eat so much junk."

When it comes to work habits, bright lines help us preserve our energy and focus and take care of what is important to us outside of work. Knowing we can cover all of our obligations means that during work hours, we can bring more of ourselves to the task.

It's important that the listener hear the other person's boundaries and ask only clarifying questions to understand them. This is not the time to argue about what's going to happen, quarrel about what has happened, or make judgmental comments. This is a time to listen and allow each speaker to get clear.

Another kind of boundary we might explore at this point is shared agreements. These can be guardrails inside of which the team or individuals are empowered to act without seeking approval, such as spending limits or domains of authority.

They can also be shared working agreements that address a specific concern.

For instance, if we're concerned that there is more work to do than time allows, then we might set a boundary that we'll prioritize together the "must-haves" for this project before we get started.

Or, if we're concerned that staff from other parts of the organization might be hostile to our project, we might set a boundary that we'll proactively reach out to other leaders to make sure they are on board.

Or, if we're concerned that we'll overspend, we could set a boundary to check in on the budget at the end of every week.

If you see an opportunity to suggest a shared boundary, it can be a useful, short conversational detour at this time, or you can write a note to address it later. What we don't want is for this conversation to devolve into a debate or problem-solving session. One final note: Stating boundaries is one of the hardest parts for some of us. Many women, especially, are raised to say yes and be as accommodating as possible. They might have even been penalized for drawing a boundary in the past or even raised in a home where they were taught to always agree with their elders, even to the point of enduring sexual assault.

Prompt questions for boundaries should tease out both personal self-care needs and project boundaries. Here are some ideas to get you started:

- ▶ What self-care rules will help you to do your best?
- ▶ What rules or standards will help this team to be the best?
- ▶ What are you 100 percent unwilling to do when it comes to this experience?
- ▶ What are the items this project must address?
- ▶ What should never be changed about our product/organization?

Some common personal boundaries we hear are:

- ▶ I won't work on the weekend.
- ▶ I will answer email only during work hours.
- ▶ I eat dinner at 5:00 p.m. with my family every weekday.
- ▶ I exercise three times per week on my lunch hour.
- ▶ I have to give another project at least 25 percent of my attention.

Some common project boundaries we hear are:

- ▶ Don't change compensation or lines of reporting.
- ▶ Don't change feature X in our product.
- ▶ Don't spend more than $10,000 on this effort.

You might find that stating boundaries—or even articulating them to yourself—is challenging. If this happens, try thinking of the boundaries you express in this section as "starter boundaries." Take pressure off yourself—you don't have to get them perfect the first time.

Instead, try to get out a few ideas that are good enough for now. And remember that you can always revisit the topic later to refine or change your stated boundaries.

In many ways, boundaries are the crux of the whole conversation and often the most unfamiliar to people going through the exercise for the first time.

As you have more practice using AIM, you will become more comfortable hearing about other people's boundaries and sharing your own. It is a vital life skill from which many of us can benefit.

Shared Agreements

The boundary conversation naturally feeds into a conversation about shared agreements, or working agreements. These are rules or thresholds put in place to keep things on track—they help create a kind of early warning system and allow time for course correction.

At times, these rules are so self-evident and cost so little that they are easy to implement. If that is the case, feel free to make note of them during the conversation. However, often careful thought and negotiation are needed to figure out the best rules and reach agreement on their implementation. In this case, you should have a separate conversation after you have completed AIM.

To articulate and create shared agreements, first think over the full all-in conversation—especially the concerns raised—and suggest simple and clear rules that could govern the project or event you are discussing.

We can make agreements about almost anything, from budgeting to communication to interpersonal interactions. Here are some we've seen put in place for work projects and at home:

- ► Pause intense conversations if anyone is hungry, tired, or intoxicated.
- ► Communicate via messaging tool (e.g., Slack) only for this project—no email.
- ► Schedule a weekly check-in to review the budget and update plans.
- ► Assume positive intent when communicating with each other.
- ► Don't spend more than X dollars without checking in with others.
- ► Make sure your calendar is up to date and visible to teammates.
- ► Take a walk each day, and get alone time when you visit family.

▸ Don't stay with challenging family members when you visit; get a hotel.

▸ Stay no more than three, and no less than two, nights in any city during a vacation.

Dreams

Let's end on a high note! You've made it through the tough parts of the conversation, and now it's time to celebrate and have fun.

It might be tempting to skip this section or give it less time than the others, but this would be a big mistake. If you want alignment, engagement, and motivation, it is better to be pulled by our shared vision of the future than simply avoiding trouble or pain. Articulating dreams will likely require more vulnerability than you think. For many, it can even be controversial to allow ourselves to hope for the best.

This section is an opportunity to let our imagination run wild and be our most ambitious or even selfish.

It's possible that none of what we desire will come true, of course, but that doesn't matter. What we want is to set our bar high and dream together of all that might happen if all goes well.

This is the time to dig deep, dream big, and speak to the situation from our authentic hearts.

Dreams are the ultimate outcomes that reflect our wishes. They might be about money, career advancement, accolades, and more. Perhaps we want to work on a project so successful that it makes industry news, or we want to build an incredible team that's asked to take on even bigger challenges next.

Prompt questions for this section should tease out the most superlative, yet grounded, outcomes imaginable. Here are some ideas for getting started:

- ▶ If this goes incredibly well, what will be true after it is over?
- ▶ How will you feel during and afterward?
- ▶ Where will you be in your life, career, or geographically?
- ▶ What business metrics will have shifted? And by how much?

Try to be as specific as possible. It can be helpful to create a visualization of what you want:

- ▶ "I'm on stage at TED talking about the success of our project."
- ▶ "I am in a beautiful café on the Amalfi Coast with my spouse, sipping champagne and celebrating my raise."
- ▶ "We are all in a meeting with the CEO and her team being asked our opinion on a critical new investment strategy."
- ▶ "We are all receiving a bonus in recognition of our contribution to the company's mission."

▶ "I'm looking around the room at all of you and feeling a sense of pride at everything we've accomplished."

▶ "I'm feeling closer to my spouse than ever and have renewed enthusiasm and energy for getting back to work."

Your dreams are your most inspiring reasons for working on this project. At their best, they provide a deep sense of purpose and hope.

Dreams are your goals combined with heart, action, and humanity.

Sharing them with each other not only inspires you and cements your alignment but also once again creates a room full of allies. We find it almost impossible to hear people's heartfelt desires without awakening in ourselves a desire for them to have that.

We truly hope that by having this conversation, you achieve your dreams and desires in both your professional and personal lives (and help others in the process, too). That's what it's all about.

CLOSING THE CONVERSATION

Now you have the lay of the land, everyone's cards are on the table, and it's time to wrap up. We call this AIM because when you finish, you should feel a sense of deep alignment (a hell, yes!) to the project or event you have discussed. And, of course, you might have also identified a mismatch on the team or in the relationship, and the outcome you are all in for is cancelling or changing things in some fundamental way.

If you are not a hell, yes, it is usually (but not always) best to be a hell, no—if that is the case, be especially gentle with the closing and generous with the break afterward.

When you are finished with the AIM conversation, it might be tempting to capture next steps or make some immediate decisions. In chapter 6, we will cover what can come after the conversation to help codify what's been learned. But the conversation actually *is* the work, and sharing in this way can bring up a lot of emotions. So, we recommend ending it with a "thank you" and a healthy break before getting into the next items.

Take a breath and recommit to your next steps with greater clarity, confidence, and compassion for everyone involved.

after the conversation

When finishing a conversation that promises radical alignment—and that has generated many thoughts and insights as well as brought up some emotions—you'll be tempted to ask, What's next?

The All-In Method (AIM) is an excellent precursor to planning a project, vacation, or event. It is also a great part of a team launch, an annual planning session, or a retrospective. But it is not a replacement for these other valuable processes and tools. It is designed to add deeper emotional and intellectual context to the next steps by creating more nuance and a feeling of interpersonal alignment.

At work, we want most meetings to end with a clear vision of next steps and who is accountable for which actions—and below we'll go over some of the more common follow-on items that AIM will generate. But consider this: the conversation *is* the work.

Radical alignment happens when we *feel* more aligned with each other, not when our project management tools are full of new tasks and initiatives.

One of the reasons we have *dreams* as the final step in AIM is that ending on a high note brings a sense of cohesion and connection to the entire process and ensures that *recency bias* works in our favor going forward.

Recency bias, as the name suggests, is the cognitive tendency to most easily remember something that just happened and not quickly call to mind things that happened further in the past. We consider dreams the perfect way to place the cherry on top of your conversation—it is the dessert, and like dessert, it should not be skipped.

After you close the conversation, there might be opportunities to articulate next steps and decide which insights to bring forward. But don't feel pressure to do this.

Sometimes specific items will simply be the self-evident shared agreements mentioned earlier. These are put in place to address a specific concern—such as a weekly budget check-in to prevent cost overrun.

And in other cases, AIM generates information that could indicate the need or opportunity for a big new project. For example, everyone in the conversation could articulate dreams of a profound disruption to a particular product space and realize you need to develop new team structures and practices that allow for more regular customer engagement and also need to hire an experienced designer to make this happen. Initiatives of this size and complexity are not suitable to address with a closing round.

In many cases, tying up the conversation into a neat bow might be impossible. AIM is designed to bring information to the surface and create rich interpersonal connections. The intent is to develop more psychological safety and trust and therefore gain more nuanced and better information. This is complex work and might not be easily summarized in bullet points and plans.

That said, possible concrete next steps can come out of AIM. Although we don't advocate for forcing specific outcomes, it is good to be aware of the possibilities.

Conscious Closing

The first step you should take to close is to thank each other for the care, attention, and vulnerability this conversation requires. Taking even a moment to savor what just happened can let the lessons sink in and become real.

You might also invite reflection from all the participants in the conversation: What did you learn? What stood out? How do you feel now, and how is that different from when we started?

If appropriate and necessary, you can then move on to a review of any agreements, new boundaries, and timelines for any actions you've committed to.

Clearly stating what you've discovered and what you are planning as individuals and as a group becomes a sort of closing ritual. As a couple, we immediately set any dates in our shared calendar. With teams, we use a reliable project management strategy of sending out a one-page summary of agreements and/or updating a shared project tool such as

Trello or Asana. We make sure that each next step has an owner and that someone is responsible for tracking and following up on action items.

Choose a date that makes sense for the individuals and the project and remind people that they can negotiate on when they will fulfill their agreement. We love specificity, such as the phrase, "I'll do task X by day Y," but this isn't the time to force things.

You aren't helicopter parents to each other, and people generally don't enjoy being watched. Don't let the tracking turn you into a micromanager. Be as compassionate as possible. People on your team have complex lives, responsibilities, and relationships. In organizations, people are usually working on more than one team and usually report to more than one person—you're probably not the only person asking for their time.

Using AIM helps you to better understand their current reality, building natural empathy, accountability, and respect.

POSSIBLE OUTCOMES

Broadly speaking, there are three ways your conversation might end. All three outcomes are positive and acceptable. Remember, the goal is not to force alignment or coerce compliance but to discover where alignment exists and make plans with everyone's needs in mind.

These are energetic and feeling-based distinctions:

- **A clear and obvious yes:** In this case, everyone at the end of the conversation feels 100 percent aligned, clear, and ready to move forward. So, go forth and enjoy the experience, begin the project, or work on your shared plan. No further discussion is needed at this point. If this is the case for you, and we hope it is, congratulations! Celebrate and move on.

- **A clear and obvious no:** Here, you've discovered that you're not at all aligned and agree not to move forward together. So, cancel, delay, and separate. And once again, no further discussion is needed. It's also appropriate to mutually agree to take some time and revisit the conversation in the future. Choose a tentative time, whether it is two days or two weeks away or in the next quarter. It might feel counterintuitive, but it is also useful to celebrate this outcome and move on.

- **An opportunity for negotiation and mitigation:** This middle ground is the most challenging place to end a conversation. Here, you not only have an understanding (hopefully shared) that everyone is not 100 percent aligned but also a sense that there is room to improve your plan and meet everyone's needs so you can still move forward.

It is also possible that more information or time is needed to become clear. In this case you might agree to delay the start of the project or put off finalizing a plan for a vacation and come back together at a specific time to discuss it again and definitively move forward or backward.

Further, there might be a few specific items that require further processing. In these cases, you might want to move to other tools and facilitated methodologies. Let's look at the types of tensions that can arise or, more accurately, become visible through the process, and what you might do about them.

The point of AIM is to make more of the relational iceberg visible. This allows you to see beneath the surface to more essential misalignments and disagreements and to project forward in time to see possible future problems before they are upon you and have become intractable and expensive to deal with.

You Can See Clearly Now

The information you gain using AIM might lead you to create some new agreements. Because clarity and boundaries tend to improve personal and professional relationships, paths you might want to get clear on are exposed even further. Each of the items that arise has a body of work that sits behind it.

You might want to employ a facilitated process to formalize boundaries and agreements. This practice can be part of a larger team-chartering process. AIM is a great opener for team or project-chartering meetings as well as quarterly or annual planning.

A few options:

▶ Designate a facilitator from the team to create a set of agreements.
▶ When having the conversation in our marriage, we often sum up the boundaries and next steps that become clear.
▶ When having the conversation with a team that has no facilitator, decide as a group if you will use AIM for clarity or goal setting at the beginning.

Working Agreements

A working agreement is any explicit standard members of a team or couple sets that helps them create the kind of collaborative space and culture they want to. A useful phrase defining culture is "the way things are done around here," and one way to improve that culture is to create new working agreements that alter the way things are done. Even a household or neighborhood has a culture.

If you want better communication between two or more people, then creating a regular cadence of specialized touchpoints—meetings and tools—is one way to improve it. In our marriage, we schedule monthly "money and planning" meetings in which we use AIM to guide us. Working agreements are often used to articulate the cadence and agendas of standing team meetings, where work is done, how it is shared (Google docs, Sharepoint, etc.), how it is tracked (what tool is used and who is responsible for keeping it updated), and work hours (when people are expected to be available or in the office—assuming you have one).

Roles and Accountabilities

When it comes to working in a volatile, uncertain, complex, and ambiguous (VUCA) world, it's useful to get clear about individual roles and accountabilities. We believe that most often in a "roles, not souls" approach, any individual might inhabit more than one role, and a role is not necessarily synonymous with the title that appears on the organizational chart. Roles can even rotate among individuals.

In a personal relationship, it's helpful for each person to take responsibility for different aspects or roles. Having clarity about who is in charge of specific tasks has saved us from many arguments!

Often teams or couples will discover through AIM that they have been unclear about who is responsible for specific decisions and, if the decision is a shared one, how this shared process is approached.

Each role should have a name and a set of outcome-focused accountabilities. For instance, a project manager role could be accountable for

▶ scheduling and facilitating planning meetings;
▶ ensuring the project management tool is up to date; and
▶ being aware of how much each person is working, spotting people who are overworked, and helping rectify that situation.

If you already use this framework, AIM might give you information that helps you edit and improve it.

If you don't use it, you might discover that many people are concerned about overwork and tasks falling through the cracks, and this might indicate you need to do a session in which this is articulated.

WHEN THINGS FALL APART

Although we consider AIM pretty magical, it's not 100 percent guaranteed to work in every situation. People will argue or go off track, or the conversation might stall because of any number of factors. What do you do next if things start to fall apart?

If you can't come into alignment, meaning you aren't all *all in,* try to get to the root of what's stalling the agreement. Is there one particular point you don't know how to react to? Does someone have a new boundary that's throwing other people off? Are you getting derailed by an old or unrelated issue coming up in the conversation?

We use the same method to burrow into the most specific trouble spot we can. Is there a new boundary or concern that is getting everyone's attention, or even just causing one person great anxiety? Go deeper into that one topic before returning to the larger topic.

We introduced the method to our friends Kate Northrup and Mike Watts. This married couple runs a family-owned, online business together. Kate teaches, writes, and runs coaching programs for women, and Mike manages the organizational structure and technical aspects of the business and consults with other entrepreneurs on their strategies. While using the method for interviewing new hires and running annual reviews for employees, they stumbled on a deeper question that needed to be addressed: Did they want to continue working together in their business?

> We were talking about our roles and structure within the company and realized we needed to talk about whether we even wanted to work together! We used it to make sure that nothing was left unsaid. In the past I've found myself having these big, important conversations and then I walk away from it and I'm like, "Oh no!" We didn't address something. And if you're gonna make a big decision based on a conversation and not everything is being said, obviously that's a problem. I like how it gets into the corners to make sure that the cobwebs are swept out.

In an annual review with a team member, Kate realized her employee Elisia wasn't happy: "I realized during that conversation how stressed out she was and how her current role was not serving her and how much her gifts and talents were not being utilized." Using the framework, Kate and Mike were able to address the specifics of the new problems that came to light and come into alignment about new boundaries in Elisia's role.

Using this method from the beginning helps you avoid common pitfalls in conversations. You've been clear about the intention from the start. It's also helpful to have one person designated to facilitate the conversation in a couple or group.

This meeting in the middle is best done by generating shared boundaries and working agreements. The intention here is to make the project, or some small aspect of it, "safe to try" for everyone. The reason we emphasize safety rather than surety is that almost all valuable experiences in life involve some degree of risk. Our goal isn't to remove risk entirely but to create a sense of shared safety in risk-taking.

And, of course, in some truly challenging conversations such as those involving divorce, business contracts, and the like, you might want to engage a mediator or facilitator to help keep the conversation clear and focused.

You might also need to use other processes and tools. This conversation is not designed for adversarial negotiations in which each party is trying to maximize their own outcome. It's meant for environments in which both parties really want to be aligned and are feeling friendly, or at least willing to feel friendly, toward each other.

In many cases, you'll be able to reach agreement on shared boundaries organically—often, this accord happens during the course of AIM without a formal process or even much discussion.

Although yes usually feels good and no usually feels bad, both are preferable to vagueness. So, keep going until you feel sure of your own yes and the yes of everyone involved.

MEETING WRAP-UP TIPS AND BEST PRACTICES

How you end your meetings is as important as how you begin them. In our consulting work as well as our marriage, we've seen that the "dessert," or "aftertaste," of a conversation can make or break the future of the agreements and insights gleaned from it.

Here are five ways to end conversations positively, with direction and group commitment:

1. **Keep it positive.** Each person shares a positive highlight from another person's contributions. This is a "make everyone feel valued" moment. Try to make sure all participants are recognized and leave with some acknowledgment that they contributed to the conversation or group as a whole. If you led the conversation, let the others know how successful you feel the meeting was, even if it means highlighting just one good moment or result.

2. **Honor the difficulty you all faced.** Some conversations end with hurt feelings. For change to occur, people have to make changes, and humans don't always love change. It takes bravery and resilience to try things in a new way.

If you have a conversation that gets contentious, end the meeting by acknowledging what is and isn't working and honoring the hurt feelings before going on to the next steps.

3. **Recognize the optimism.** If people were willing to take risks, try new ideas, and think outside the box, point out their commitment to optimism. This is a key ingredient in engagement, creativity, and innovation, and every team, couple, and company needs more optimism. Encourage the optimism you witnessed in the conversation by supporting ongoing experimentation and sharing of intentions, concerns, boundaries, and especially dreams.

4. **Highlight the dreams.** The human need to understand how we contribute to the success of a project, relationship, or organization gives us a sense of meaning and purpose. Highlight the shared dreams of the attendees by explaining exactly how each person's dreams fit into the larger project or relationship.

5. **Commit to action.** Toward the end of your meeting, briefly list the action steps that will take place next. Remind everyone where the project is headed—outline the big picture. End it with genuine warmth, and express gratitude.

Seeing the Relational Iceberg

In reality, disagreements between people are going to persist no matter what conversation they have. This is part of the challenge and the opportunity in collaboration and sharing experiences with others. We might think disagreements are a problem to be solved, but really, they are a feature of every healthy human interaction.

We want diverse teams at work because they have different perspectives and ideas—and more than that, the conflict that naturally arises can actually push a team toward more creative solutions. We think innovation is adding perspective A to perspective B. But really, A and B bumping into each other and even annoying each other forces the creation of the brand-new perspective everyone can now share.

In our home, Bob brings a certain orderly and systems-focused perspective, and Alex brings an artistic and organic one—with plants and cats and art projects—that together create a home and a life that neither of us is capable of on our own. The result is a cozy home that we love and that enriches both of our lives. But this happens because of our differences and our disagreements.

By taking time to share deeply with each other, we build bonds that go beyond simple plans, tools, and agreements. We build a basis for deeper understanding, forgiveness, and trust. This is the real promise of radical alignment and AIM.

What looks on the surface like a simple tool to plan an event is actually an opportunity for deeper, more human, and more real connections.

Maria Popova echoes this sentiment in a way we love: "The richest relationships are lifeboats, but they are also submarines that descend to the darkest and most disquieting places, to the unfathomed trenches of the soul where our deepest shames and foibles and vulnerabilities live, where we are less than we would like to be."

We find AIM to be a kind of Trojan horse. We invite it in as a simple, linear process to straighten out a plan, but over time it can open up much more than we intended and bring down our defenses.

all-in at work

AT WORK, the All-In Method (AIM) will help make emotional conversations more linear and therefore both safer and more likely to happen. It is increasingly essential to have emotional conversations at work because collaboration is now an essential component of most jobs—and working together, whether we like it or not, is an emotional experience.

Liz Fosslien and Molly West Duffy put it this way in *No Hard Feelings: The Secret Power of Embracing Emotions at Work*: "Humans are emotional creatures, regardless of circumstance. By ignoring our feelings at work, we overlook important data and risk making preventable mistakes. We send emails that cause unnecessary anxiety, we fail to find work meaningful, and we burn out."[1]

This means that coercive, command-and-control styles of leadership—at work, in a neighborhood, a community, or even at home—are not only immoral but also impractical. In fast-moving times, we need all hands on deck and all brains engaged. Manipulative and charisma-driven leadership are being replaced with empathy-building conversations. Some of the best leaders are, in fact, the most relational and the humblest.

Although this might sound like touchy-feely nonsense to hard-nosed traditionalists, consider that General Stanley McChrystal—former leader of the Joint Special Operations Command (JSOC) and commander of the US forces in Afghanistan—advocates for leaders to become more like gardeners. This, he says, has more to do with tending and empowering people than it does with being directive, making decisions, and giving orders.[2]

Psychologist Terry Real sums up the mindset of the twenty-first-century leader like this: "You're not above the system, you're a humble sub-component part of the system. You live inside of it. And it's in your interest to keep it clean and healthy."[3]

There is a need for modern leaders to be emotionally adept—able to be appropriately vulnerable themselves and to nurture healthy emotional landscapes for their teams. AIM is a great place to start if you want to change your communication style to focus more on relationships and empathy.

Aaron Dignan, in *Brave New Work*, uses AIM with clients of his consulting firm, The Ready, for projects that require what he calls "cognitive divergence" or that are experiencing a "lack of vulnerability and connection."

Nadir Ahmad, founder and CEO of the consulting firm Dowling Street, says AIM generates "vulnerability without the risk" and that it is "good for 'left-brained' people because when you ask people to kind of step into this process with you, you give them an action orientation so that it feels very inviting. It feels very comfortable."

Now we'll go deep into how AIM plays out in specific professional situations. We'll refer to two distinct types of scenarios: *facilitated use* and *one-sided use*.

Facilitated use refers to situations in which attendees agree to and are aware that they are participating in a structured conversation.

One-sided use refers to situations in which one person is aware of the structure, but the other person is not. This can be done subtly without the other person or people even knowing a method is being applied. It is also fine to let the other person know you will be guiding the conversation using a script. However, that might not always be necessary or helpful.

The Project Launch

Bob first began using AIM in business when working on consulting teams. The first use was with the consulting team itself. In consulting firms, new teams are often formed to begin a new project, and he found that AIM is a valuable way to get the team up to speed quickly and to connect.

Later he realized that clients too could benefit from the method because projects that require outside consulting are usually high stakes and high risk. Consultants are expensive and brought in only when there is a lot of risk, a lot of opportunities, or both.

When Bob and his business partner, Lisa Lewin, started a firm, the first thing they did was to go through AIM together. And we (Alex and Bob) have used AIM in a variety of contexts over the years, from work with schools to theater to nonprofits and community groups. When we say *work,* we mean anytime a group is coming together for a project, not just corporate or profit-driven enterprises.

When using AIM to kick off a team, bring everyone together for a couple of hours and go through the process step by step. This is a good precursor to a team-chartering exercise (the appendix has a guide to this), so you can take care of both the emotional (intelligence) quotient (EQ) and the intelligence quotient (IQ) of the team. It is best to do this in neutral territory, away from the office.

The most valuable facilitation method we've found is to have people "journal" their answers onto Post-it® notes (one idea per note), then share them one at a time as they place their notes on a specific section of wall, whiteboard, or a flip-chart panel associated with that section—gathering all intentions in one spot, concerns in another, and so forth.

AIM Prompts for Launching Projects

As with anytime you use AIM, getting the prompt question right is important and should be customized to your situation. Below are some ideas to get you started.

> ▶ **Intentions:** Why are we doing this project? Why did you choose to be a part of it? Notice that we are focused on both the project's intention and each person's individual reasons for being a part of it.

▶ **Concerns:** Given our team structure, resources, and goals, what worries you about this project? If this project fails, why do you think it will have failed? This is where you are pulling out the design criteria and looking for flaws in it.

▶ **Boundaries:** What do you need to be successful at work? How much time can you devote to this project? What rules or agreements can we make that will keep us being the most productive and help us avoid risks? Boundaries for work projects should cover what each individual needs because work styles and time allocation might vary considerably between individuals. It should also cover agreements the team can make with each other and practices that members can adopt in order to live their values and keep the project on track.

▶ **Dreams:** How will we know if this project is wildly successful? What will be true for you if it is? Again, we want to tease out and invite both an individual focus and a project focus. A wildly successful project can generate money and impact at the organizational level, and it can open up new possibilities for the individuals involved.

PROJECT PLANNING

Markets, technology, and culture today seem to be in a state of almost continuous change. Organizations able to operate in this volatile, uncertain, complex, and ambiguous (VUCA) environment tend to plan, and replan, on a much more frequent basis than businesses did just a decade ago.

A management practice Bob frequently implements with his clients—whether the "project" is running an entire company or producing a small product feature—is a regular cadence of looking back and looking forward. The look back is usually called a *retrospective,* and the look forward is *planning*—whether annual, quarterly, or even monthly in some cases.

A retrospective can take on many formats, but they all follow the same three steps:

1. **Gather data** (qualitative and quantitative) about what happened over a specific time period.
2. **Generate insights** about possible causes and improvements that could be made to processes and team dynamics.
3. **Adopt changes** that you think will make a difference.

The frequency and scope of the retrospective/planning cadence should be customized to the size of the team and the complexity of a project. If the project has a lot of moving parts, risk, and uncertainty, then it will benefit from a small and dedicated team. Projects like this are common in software development, and weekly or biweekly planning in this case is valuable.

For larger groups or entire organizations, a retrospective and planning cycle could happen on a less frequent cadence, such as quarterly planning and/or annual planning. You can get Bob's guide to retrospectives in our Extras pack on our website.

AIM fits well between a retrospective and planning. It helps the team digest what has been covered in the look back and sets the stage for looking forward toward the next phase of the project or business. It also allows for team members to express and process emotions—this is especially important if the retrospective was a difficult one.

AIM Prompts for Planning Projects

We usually start a planning process by having the project leader(s) state the goals for the next period (e.g., month, quarter, or year) to constrain AIM to a specific set of goals and time frame.

Prompt questions for AIM should be designed to help members articulate their personal connection to the project success and identify possible roadblocks to that success. Here are some ideas to get you started:

- ▶ **Intentions:** What are we working toward in the next [period]? What do we intend to accomplish? For planning, we are usually focused on the shared goals of the team, but this exercise gives people a chance to add some detail and color to the broader goals. The business goals might be high level, such as "launch v2.3 of our product," but the team will have much more information about what must be done to make that happen. You might be part of a small group working on a class project, a collective of artists working toward a group show, or a nonprofit focused on a fundraiser.

▶ **Concerns:** Given our team structure, resources, and goals, what worries you about the next phase of this project? If this project fails, why do you think it will have failed?

▶ **Boundaries:** What do you personally need to be successful? How much time can you devote to this project? What rules or agreements can we make that will keep us most productive and help us avoid risks? Although these boundaries might have been stated at the beginning of the project—the prompts are identical, in fact—new information will likely have emerged over time, and restating boundaries is never a bad idea.

▶ **Dreams:** How will we know if this project is wildly successful? What will be true for you if it is? Again, these are identical to the prompts for the project launch, but we want to restate and reinspire ourselves even if nothing has changed. And it is likely new insights and information will have emerged since the project started.

Hiring/Onboarding New Employees

There appears to be a power dynamic in hiring—the employer holds all the cards. But that is only true if the candidate has no other options. Great candidates for any job will have several options. Competition for talent in many industries is a big issue.

Even if your business has a monopoly on jobs in a region or industry, you still want to hire the person who is the best match for the job. And you will want to set up the new employee for success, which means building a foundation of two-way communication and care.

We've seen several businesses have success with using AIM as part of the interview process.

Having a script for hiring conversations can help minimize bias, and although we believe AIM is a good starting place for the conversation, it should not be the whole of your hiring process.

AIM Prompts for Hiring

We find it best if the person doing the interview goes first, and the candidate goes second.

> ▶ **Intentions:** We are hiring for this position because [of this gap in skills or capacity on our team]. What is important to you when it comes to a job? Why would you want to work here?

▶ **Concerns:** It is important to us that we find someone who [has these specific skills or characteristics and embodies these qualities]. What worries do you have going into a new job? Are there any concerns you have specific to this opportunity, given what you know about it?

▶ **Boundaries:** This job involves [these work hours and these accountabilities]. We also expect. . . . What do you need to be successful at work? What working agreements have helped you be successful on teams in the past? What do you find important and restorative outside of work?

▶ **Dreams:** We hope you find a place here and stay for a very long time. If this job is wildly successful for you, what will be true in one year? In five years?

Job Interviewing

Interviewing for a job might be one of the most unnatural experiences we endure as humans. To come across as genuine, put your best self forward, manage your physical and energetic presence, and also offer your past accomplishments without seeming like you're on a first date is quite a balancing act.

Using AIM to help you examine a potential employer and position from all angles can help your interviewer see you as the right fit for the job. Employers tend to favor candidates who are curious about and actively interested in the position.

It can also help you determine if the job is a good fit for you—we too often forget to do this!

AIM Prompts for Job Interviewing
Here are a few ways you can use AIM to guide your interaction as an interviewee so you come across as the thoughtful team player you are:

- ▶ **Intentions:** Why are you looking to hire someone for this position? Are you expanding, restructuring, or did someone leave? Tell me about the opportunities for training in this position.
- ▶ **Concerns:** Tell me about people who have not been a fit (e.g., a bad hire).
- ▶ **Boundaries:** What are the weekend and after-work expectations for responding to email? Are there offsite gatherings or team meetings?
- ▶ **Dreams:** What are the growth opportunities here? Imagine it's a year from now, and we're in my year-end review: What will have happened in that year to have you feel like this was a great hire?

RELATIONSHIP RESET

AIM can also be used to review and reset an employee/employer relationship. Kate Northrup used it to reestablish a quality working relationship with her company's head of operations. She says, "The conversation made it clear that we did want to work together, but her role needed to change. She had been running our company for over a year—we were just in a new season of life and business. She was overworked, and we didn't realize it. And she was freaking stressed out."

Sales

The idea that everyone is in sales, whether you're a professional salesperson or not, has recently gained a lot of traction. Students need to promote their ideas and prove their thesis to a teacher or classmates. Nonprofit organizations are constantly working to influence donors and entice partners to lend their names and resources to a cause. Parents are constantly putting forth ideas in a way to get their children to align with the rules. And authors are selling publishers on their next project. In short, we are all salespeople now.

Neither of us started off our careers as salespeople, and we both have had to overcome our disdain for the process— perhaps when we were growing up in the 1980s, we watched too many movies in which the villain was a businessman and all salespeople were slimy.

Realizing that sales are really about relationship building and matchmaking made all the difference. Also, reputation is everything and a force multiplier when it comes to sales. This means we are committed to making sure both parties believe a deal is a win (e.g., they are radically aligned).

The steps of any successful sales process involve

- ▶ getting to know the prospective client,
- ▶ deciding if client and product are a good fit, and
- ▶ closing the deal.

Using AIM has become part of our sales process, whether for large-scale corporate consulting or one-on-one coaching for entrepreneurs. It helps us stay focused on the customer instead of ourselves. The worst salespeople want to make a sale for their own gain, and the best are there to facilitate the most advantageous outcome for the prospect, whether that is a sale, a referral to someone else, or a pass.

AIM keeps us curious and focused on the relationship, not the outcome, and this makes the sales process so much more pleasurable for all involved.

Because we sell services, the examples below are primarily focused on a services sale. But they can easily be adapted to product sales.

AIM Prompts for Sales
We use intentions, concerns, boundaries, and dreams to help understand our prospect's challenges and desired outcomes. We find that delving into each of the four areas helps uncover the true motivations, fears, and desires of a client. Here are examples of questions we have asked in sales conversations:

- ▶ **Intentions:** Why are you seeking coaching now? Why are we talking today? Why have you chosen to talk with me in particular; are there other coaches you've spoken with, or is there something about my work in particular you're interested in? What problems are you facing that you'd like to fix?

- ▶ **Concerns:** What challenges or obstacles do you see in the way of achieving your goals? What concerns do you have about working with a coach? Have you worked with a coach in the past, and if so, how satisfied were you with the outcomes? It's two years from now, and things have gone poorly—what went wrong?

- ▶ **Boundaries:** Are there areas of your life or work you don't want to bring into coaching? What times and days are you available? What do you need to make coaching work best for you; do you prefer virtual coaching via phone or video chat, or do you require in-person appointments?

- ▶ **Dreams:** It's a year in the future, and this coaching or consulting work has gone beautifully; what would have happened for you to be 100 percent satisfied? How will your life look and feel when you achieve your desired outcomes?

In *Never Split the Difference*, Chris Voss, lead hostage negotiator for the Federal Bureau of Investigation (FBI), outlines his theory of *tactical empathy*. This is simply focusing in and discovering what the other person wants. AIM is essentially a four-part conversation to help you understand what the other person wants so you can decide if you can offer it or help them get it.

We find that after thirty minutes or an hour talking with a prospect using AIM, we are able to confidently move forward with the sales process or pass on it.

Moderating Panels

Both of us have had the pleasure of guiding group conversations in front of an audience, usually for conferences, daylong workshops, or other sponsored events. We love moderating panels! Guiding important conversations with experts to educate and inspire a room is a thrill. Although some people feel that being asked to moderate a panel is "coming in second place," we feel it's a golden opportunity to bring out the best in the panelists and ask burning questions of our own.

Knowing how to easily and effectively organize a panel discussion is a powerful skill to have on the road to positioning yourself as an expert. Good moderators ask questions that highlight the strengths of the panelists; excellent moderators work to make each panelist, and themselves, look like geniuses.

AIM Prompts for Moderating Panels

Being a great listener and having the ability to veer off script keeps panels engaging and powerful. Bob recently discovered that AIM worked well to organize his questions and flow for a panel on the future of work. Here's an example of the questions he posed:

- ▶ **Intentions:** Why did you decide to come and speak at this conference? Why is this topic so important to you?
- ▶ **Concerns:** What concerns do you have about the future of work? What mistakes do you see people making that negatively affect the work you do?
- ▶ **Boundaries:** What do you make sure not to do in your work? How do you best take care of yourself in volatile situations during your projects?
- ▶ **Dreams:** What is the best possible future you envision for your work?

Use AIM to help create psychological safety even in a panel setting, giving each speaker the same questions to answer. The method allows the guests to share their emotions and passions as well as their EQ and IQ, which makes for a much more interesting event. On our website, you can see a video of Bob using AIM to moderate a panel.

Planning a Speech

Most people dread giving a live speech—according to some research, the fear of public speaking ranks higher than the fear of death. Yet at nearly every stage of life and work, we are called on to offer our ideas in public. Students need to present reports for school projects, artists stand in front of their work for critical reviews and gallery presentations, and employees often need to ask questions or raise concerns in staff meetings. All of these occasions can be considered speeches, and people can use AIM to help them prepare to voice their truth.

We both regularly give keynote talks to audiences as part of our work. This is a particular kind of sales because talks always involve some degree of customization. If you want a talk to go well, it is important for you to understand the audience and the goals of the organizer. A little bit of empathy goes a long way.

AIM Prompts for Speech Planning

Here are some questions we ask of any organizer we are working with to plan our speeches:

- ► **Intentions:** Why are you running the conference or event? Why are people attending the event? What do they hope to get out of the day? What are the goals this event will contribute to achieving? Who are they, and are they paying to attend?
- ► **Concerns:** What might go wrong at the event? Have you ever had a bad or damaging person speak? What happened? Why?
- ► **Boundaries:** Are there any topics we should avoid during the talk? What is the room like? Will I be able to see the audience? How many people will be in the

room? What time of day am I speaking? Is it okay to ask questions of the audience or ask them to interact with each other in a workshop-like activity? How does your audience feel about the use of (mild) profanity?

▶ **Dreams:** Can you tell me about the best speakers you've had on stage? What made them great? If I'm really great, how will you know? What will be true?

Asking these questions accomplishes two objectives. First, you get valuable information that can help you tailor your talk and activities to make them directly relevant to the audience. Audiences love feeling special, and demonstrating to them that you know who they are and what they care about is incredibly valuable. Second, it makes the conference organizers feel they are important and have been heard by you. Great speakers build strong relationships with organizers, in our experience. That's how you'll get invited back and referred to other venues.

DEALING WITH A DOWNTURN

Aaron Dignan had one of his most notable experiences with AIM with the marketing leadership team at a Fortune 50 company. The members of this team had just come out of some layoffs that had resulted in significant cuts to their head count. He led the conversation at the start of an offsite meeting for about thirty people, asking them to journal first on each topic. They then sat in a circle, and each person in turn shared their one- or two-sentence answer; it took about ninety minutes to get through the full team's statements.

Although this might sound like a lot of people and a long session, Dignan says, "I think it was just really centering for everyone because they got to express their vulnerability and their fear and their anxiety and hear it replicated over and over and over again. So, there was a feeling of community in the experience and emotional support—like we're all in this together."

We are sure there are many other circumstances in which AIM can be useful. Please go to our website to share what you learn and to learn from others!

Although we don't cover it in the steps above, you can also use AIM by yourself as a journaling method to get clear yourself before beginning a conversation with another person.

8

all-in at home

ALTHOUGH THE ALL-IN METHOD (AIM) has been revolutionary for us and many others in work settings, we find it perhaps most impactful in our personal relationships.

We are both community builders and connection makers, so we value our networks of personal relationships above anything else we have created in our lives. And our marriage sits at the center of this—it is both the beneficiary of rich social connections and a source of them.

When we met almost a decade ago, we both had a history of difficult relationships behind us. Bob had been married three times and Alex once.

We decided at that time to be deliberate about creating a relationship that served us both, in addition to coparenting Alex's young son from her first marriage. We were fortunate to be incredibly compatible in disposition and desires, but all relationships take work, and we leaned into it.

AIM was something we applied early on to discussions about family trips and moving in together, and eventually we used it to discuss marriage, coparenting, retirement investing together, and even pre-funeral needs.

Esther Perel, a couple's therapist, once told us that if we stayed together for a long time, we would have more than one relationship with each other, and we'd have to be prepared to allow our relationship to evolve. We find that expecting our relationship to change and having practices to return to when change or reevaluation is needed has been a central feature of creating a relationship that, after more than eight years, is still deeply rewarding, pleasurable, and supportive for us both.

AIM is now part of our relationship in the same way that playing scales are a part of jazz improvisation. Sometimes we return to the method and have a structured conversation with each other, but more often than not some part of AIM will simply appear in an interaction. Because we have practiced the full method so often, we now have a shared vocabulary that allows us to highlight an intention, concern, boundary, or dream in the moment. Having this shared vocabulary and way of connecting, we're fairly certain we've avoided many arguments, misunderstandings, and frustrating scenarios:

"Hey, I just realized why I want to go on this vacation."

"I'm really concerned about this."

"I just discovered a new boundary I have when it comes to work."

"My dream for this book is . . ."

That's right! We have had multiple AIM sessions around this book you are reading because it is both a business project—the first we've ever done together—and a core aspect of our relationship.

We've also used AIM to get clear about friendships, prepare for mediation with an ex-spouse, and navigate the high school application process with our son. We've used this framework to focus on important interactions and get into alignment with people who didn't need to know we were using a process with them.

Just as Kate Northrup described her tendency to focus too much on the positive and leave out possibly contentious thoughts, both of us are lifelong conflict avoiders. Although being a "smoother-over" has its benefits, we've come to believe that AIM helps us stop sidestepping important issues that, despite being uncomfortable, need to be addressed.

Our friend Rebekah shared that she uses the framework to help her have fair, measured conversations with her friends, family, and work partners. "AIM helps me see if I've missed something important to share, and I stop steamrolling over people."

At work AIM helps bring in an often-missing emotional element. But at home it actually helps you to be more strategic.

Discussing the "Big Three" Issues (Sex, Money, and Kids)

It can be challenging to be strategic in relationships, especially about situations that involve other people. But not all people are compatible, and often we can have a great deal of passion for people we are not suited to build a life with long term. Falling in love, having great chemistry, or having similar worldviews might be wonderful reasons to begin a relationship, but they are insufficient for long-term stability. For this you need to be aligned around your collective goals and intentions—and have similar life dreams.

Sex, money, and children are the cause of most relationship strife. If you want to get serious with someone, we recommend having conversations about these stickier issues early and often. AIM provides a safe structure for that conversation.

You can use the sample prompts with a potential or current partner. It can also be quite valuable to use as a journaling method by yourself to get clear before the conversation.

Remember, we enter these conversations to develop empathy, find common ground, and design the best possible version of the relationship for the people involved. You are not taking orders or "ordering off the menu." You might not get what you ask for, and you might discover you are incompatible, and it would be better to end the relationship than to pursue it further.

You might discover you are more aligned than you imagined and inspire each other, and you are ready to move forward with an intimate, shared clarity. Each time we have approached a big issue, one or both of us has some level of fear that speaking up about what we need or want will cause a rift in the relationship. But we've found the opposite to be true. Speaking up, sharing, and risking it all have led to a deeper, more aligned connection, more empathy, and more sustainability.

AIM Prompts for Sex

Below are some prompts to get you started talking about sex:

▶ **Intentions:** Why do you enjoy having sex? Connection? Pleasure? Adventure? What do you get out of it personally? What makes for a great sex life in your world?

▶ **Concerns:** When it comes to sex, what are you most worried about? Frequency? Sexually transmitted illnesses? Betrayal? What scares you?

▶ **Boundaries:** What do you know about yourself sexually? What works for you, and what doesn't? What are your deal breakers when it comes to a sexual relationship? Must you be monogamous? Which acts are must-haves in your sex life, and which are never up for consideration? What might you like to try? What are you not open to experimenting with?

▶ **Dreams:** If you are on your deathbed looking back on your life, what do you hope to be able to say about your sex life? Describe the most satisfying sexual relationship you can imagine.

AIM Prompts for Money

Below are some prompts to get you started talking about money:

▶ **Intentions:** What does money do for you? Why do you want to earn it? Do you want to be rich or just to get by?

▶ **Concerns:** What scares you about money? What negative financial messages did you absorb from childhood? Are you worried you won't have enough? That you won't appear generous? That you'll be shamed for being poor or rich?

▶ **Boundaries:** Where does money fit in your life? How much focus do you want to put on it? How much is enough for you to retire? Are you willing to do things you hate in order to earn it? What, if anything, are you willing to sacrifice in order to reach your financial goals?

▶ **Dreams:** Describe an abundant life to me—not just how much money you have in your bank account but what you are able to do with it. How do you live? If your money were abundant, what would your life look and feel like?

AIM Prompts for Having, or Coparenting, Kids

▶ **Intentions:** Why do you want to have kids? What do you imagine they will do for your life? Why do you want to parent a child together?

▶ **Concerns:** What, specifically, scares you about being a parent? Are there ways you were parented that you want to avoid passing down to your children? How do you want to divide parenting responsibilities such as discipline and meal preparation? What if you have a child who is gender nonconforming, transgendered, or gay?

What if you can't get pregnant easily or have your own children naturally?

▶ **Boundaries:** How many kids do you want to have? Where do you want to live when you have kids? What must you accomplish before you have kids? Do you want pets and children at the same time? If so, what kind of animals are acceptable and how many? Do you believe in physically disciplining children?

▶ **Dreams:** What is the ideal scenario for raising kids in your world? Describe some perfect days with your kids at different ages in their lives: birth, elementary school, middle school, high school, college, their wedding, and so forth.

CREATING REWARDING EVENTS

Often, we jump into attending or hosting events without giving much thought to our goals. The goals, and therefore the design criteria, for having a party or going on vacation might seem to be self-evident, only to fall apart upon examination.

Yehudi M. used AIM to help design his wedding. After the engagement, he gathered his parents, his in-laws to be, and his fiancée around the dining room table to discuss the event.

This was to be a family affair, and he found that although he and his bride simply wanted to be married, his parents and his in-laws had different needs. His parents wanted to be good hosts—which meant feeding people well and taking care of their needs—but this was less important to the bride and groom, who figured people could just take care of themselves.

What they discovered during the conversation brought them closer as a family and helped them have empathy for each other around spending money and logistical decisions. The conversation took only about an hour, but the groom credited it with creating a great experience for everyone involved.

AIM Prompts for Hosting a Party

Living in New York and having a wide circle of acquaintances, we get invited to a lot of events and host regular brunches and sunset parties in the warmer months on our roof deck. We love to be intentional and clear when we attend and create events. Here's how you can do it too:

- **Intentions:** Why are you having this party? What do you hope to get out of it?
- **Concerns:** What worries you about hosting this party? Too many/not enough people coming? Managing certain personalities and relationships? Running out of booze? How will you divide the planning and cleanup responsibilities?
- **Boundaries:** What are your design criteria—how many people, what will you serve, when will it end? What do

you want to make sure happens or doesn't happen at the party? What is your budget for this event? Do you encourage people to avoid talking about work or give them a few themes to talk about? Do you encourage people to talk with someone they don't know?

► **Dreams:** Looking back at the end of the party, what would you be most happy about having happened? What will make you think, "That was amazing!"?

AIM Prompts for Attending a Party

► **Intentions:** Why are you going to this party? What do you hope to get out of it? How do you want to feel when you leave?

► **Concerns:** What are you worried might or might not happen at this party? How is your energy going to the party? Maybe one of you will get tired before the other. Does one of you know more people than the other at this event? How might that affect each person's comfort level?

► **Boundaries:** What are you sure you want to experience or not experience at this party? How long do you want to stay? Will you drink alcohol at this party? If so, how many drinks is your limit? Do you not want to be left alone, or do you want to feel free to talk with other people individually? If one person is ready to go, does the other person need to leave too, or can they leave separately?

▸ **Dreams:** If this turns out to be the best party ever, what will have happened? How will you feel about each other at the end of the party if it goes really well?

VACATION OR FAMILY VISITS

Avoid the "vacation from hell" by setting yourself up for success in advance. We have used AIM before every trip since we got married and have even used it *during* a vacation when surprise changes occurred. You can use it when gathering somewhere for reunions and to prepare before family comes to stay with you.

▸ **Intentions:** What do you want out of this vacation or visit? Why do you want to go to this particular place? Why have you chosen the activities you've chosen?

▸ **Concerns:** Does one person want to relax? Do both people want to explore and be active all day? Does one person want alone time every day and worry about the other person being offended? Are you concerned about alcohol consumption on this trip or during this visit? Are other family members or friends joining? If so, do you have concerns about them?

▸ **Boundaries:** What do you need to feel your best on this vacation? What things do you prefer to avoid to feel good? Are there alcohol boundaries? Food boundaries?

Do you have a budget? Does one person not want to be left alone with certain family members? Is this a working vacation, or is work to be left at home and email avoided? What time do you want to get up in the morning or go to bed at night to feel your best?

▶ **Dreams:** If you were to come home feeling like this was your best vacation or visit yet, what would have happened to make you feel this way? How do you want to feel about your family or friends when you part ways at the end of this gathering?

WEDDING PLANNING

In our humble opinion, all weddings should use AIM! We had a wonderful experience using the format to help us create a day we loved, and we've heard from friends that it was valuable to get everyone on the same page before diving into details and spending money.

We even came up with a simple formula through which every decision was filtered: Is it high-joy and low-drama? If something (or someone) brought us joy and didn't cause drama, it was in. If not, we didn't include it in our day.

Bob's work colleague and friend Yehudi M. used AIM to guide a conversation between his parents, soon-to-be in-laws, and his fiancée. They all sat at the dining room table and went through the steps together. He said:

I wanted to start by creating space for us to talk about what we might be anxious about, what we might be excited about, and kind of how we're approaching this. I think what was really helpful is we got some big picture things out sooner rather than later. And it helped us see what was important to everyone involved in the planning. My parents were very concerned about how to take care of people traveling from overseas for the wedding, while my now-wife and I didn't care so much. I think it was less about the specifics and more about taking the time to talk about what we were trying to do together.

Whether you're planning a 200-person event or hopping over to city hall on your lunch break, here are some questions to help you get aligned:

- **Intentions:** Why do you want to have a wedding? What's your vision for this wedding? What does a wedding mean to you?
- **Concerns:** What concerns do you have about the wedding you're cocreating? What's the overall budget? What are your concerns about family or friends? Are there concerns about time management and equally handling tasks? Will you drink alcohol after? If so, how many drinks is your limit? Do you want to stay together for

the entire reception, or do you want to feel free to talk with other people individually?

► **Boundaries:** What does each person need to feel their best? What do you want to avoid doing or feeling? Are there any people you want to avoid? Any topics?

► **Dreams:** If you were to come home feeling like this was your dream wedding, what would have happened to make you feel this way? How do you want to feel about your family or friends when you part ways at the end of this gathering?

RELATIONSHIP CLARITY

Ever feel like the person you're dating has different relationship goals or expectations than yours? It's common. Your girlfriend might speak about the future in a way that doesn't line up with your vision or operate by different beliefs and rules than you hold for yourself.

How can you get clear about your partner's way of thinking, unspoken beliefs, or hopes for the future without using AIM?

Far from being manipulative, we consider this kind of conversation wise and thoughtful. After all, the best relationships are founded on clarity and honesty.

Focus the conversation as much as possible on one aspect of your relationship. It's overwhelming and unfair to address multiple topics in one sitting. Although you might have been thinking about it for a while, the other person might need time to think about responses. We've coached clients to write the four steps—*intentions, concerns, boundaries, and dreams*—on a Post-it® note and give it to their partners. Let them know a day or two before that you'd like to talk about a specific topic, that you need to find a time that works for you both, and that these are the four areas you'd like to cover.

Here are some scripted AIM prompts you can use to guide a conversation and get clear about your relationship without teaching the method first:

▶ **Intentions:** I'd like to feel like I know what you want out of our time together. I've been wondering if our expectations match up at this point. I enjoy spending time with you, and I want to feel like we can enjoy each other and also respect each other's boundaries. Are you open to having a conversation about that? What do you want out of our shared time together at this point?

▶ **Concerns:** I've noticed I'm worrying about things in my head, and I'm not sharing them with you. I don't want to hurt or upset you, but I think I need to get clear about what you're thinking so I can put these worries aside. And I'd like to hear your concerns as well. Are you open to talking about our concerns? I've found myself wondering if you're happy with the amount of time we spend together, if you feel it's too much or too little. I'm concerned that when we spend time together with other people, it's usually my friends, but not yours. I find myself having this unfounded thought that you don't want me to meet your friends, which probably isn't fair to you. What concerns do you have about what I've shared or anything else?

► **Boundaries:** I have a few thoughts about how I'd like to talk about our shared time together. With my intense work schedule, and our dating, I'm seeing I don't have as much alone time as I used to. I think I need a few hours a week to be alone and read, or hang out, or just refuel on my own. Can you think of anything you need to feel good?

► **Desires:** I would love to know what your vision is for how we spend our time together. I really enjoyed the evening walk in the park after dinner. It felt relaxed and gave us a chance to chat while letting off some steam. A few nights out a month with our mixed friends would be great—I think they'd really like each other. What's your ideal in terms of what we do, who we hang out with, and how you feel afterward?

AIM with a Parent

Our friend Justin decided to use the conversation to talk with his mother about their tense relationship. A loving, accommodating, and kind person, Justin had never expressed his grievances to his mother about how she was speaking to him and his biracial children.

The first few times he tried to talk with her about how her behavior was affecting him and his family, she was resistant to hearing what he had to say and became defensive when he tried to talk with her.

Taking her through the conversation, without even explaining they were following a format, allowed him to express his concerns in a way that she could hear them. He then gave her space to express her concerns, and over time she began to soften.

Although the relationship is still challenging, she is no longer derailing their conversations, and they have begun a new way of talking that is keeping alive the possibility of a happier, healthier connection.

Here are some examples from their conversation for you to try with your parent or relative:

- ▶ **Intentions:** Mom, I want to talk about how our relationship is so tense so we can try to make it better. My intention is for us to feel closer and for it to be easier for us to spend time together.
- ▶ **Concerns:** I'm concerned that you're going to feel bad or you're going to feel attacked. I'm concerned that you might not hear this as coming from love. I'm concerned

that my children aren't feeling safe and enjoying their
time in your home.

▶ **Boundaries:** I want my children to feel safe and loved
in your home, so please don't talk about how you don't
like their hair or clothing. I want to feel safe and loved in
your home, so please don't tell me you hate my tattoos.

▶ **Dreams:** My dream is that when we spend time together,
we all enjoy ourselves and end the family gathering with
an authentic smile on our faces.

Using AIM, Justin was finally able to say the things he
wanted to say because he wasn't being thrown off course by
the emotions of the situation. When emotions do get intense,
he has the method to return to.

Knowing what he wanted to say in advance and giving
his mom space to share her thoughts, he could just listen
and say, "Okay. I hear you on that. Now let's talk about our
boundaries." The work on their relationship continues, but
now Justin feels hopeful that real, two-way understanding is
possible. Now he understands that it's okay to point out when
situations are hurtful or aren't working. AIM has become a
way for him to remove the old judgment from the act of
self-expression and instead focus on healing and moving the
relationship forward.

Engagement/Marriage/Relationship Expansion

We weren't sure we wanted to get legally married because collectively we had enough past marriages under our belts for one lifetime. Still, we were committed to a long-term relationship, coparented a child, and had been through several health scares and surgeries in a short time, making us realize we needed some legal protections for each other. After a series of AIM conversations, we realized we did want to get married! And through our engagement, we continued to have the conversation on several topics to help us plan the wedding, get clear about housework, and more.

Couples have successfully used AIM to create clear rules and experiments for how to have ethically nonmonogamous relationships and open up to dating outside of their primary relationship. We also know people who have used AIM to have a deeper understanding of evolving gender, class, and racial dynamics within their personal—or even professional —relationships. We've also had feedback from couples who used the conversation to talk about whether to break up and how to support each other in big changes such as cross-country moves.

> ► **Intentions:** Why do you want to get married? What
> does marriage mean to you? Is being married different

from the relationship we have now? Why do you want to change how this relationship is functioning now?

▶ **Concerns:** What mistakes from past relationships or marriages do you not want to repeat in this one? Managing certain personalities and relationships? What are your needs as an introvert or an extrovert? Do you want a wedding or ceremony? (See "Wedding Planning" above in this chapter.)

▶ **Boundaries:** What do you know you need to feel good in a marriage [or however the relationship is changing]? What do you know you won't tolerate in a marriage or relationship? What are the expectations and rules around flirting with other people now and after we are married? (See "Sex" above in this chapter.)

▶ **Dreams:** If you were to look back on our marriage as one of the best things about your life, on your last day alive, what would have transpired? How do you hope our relationship will evolve as a result of this engagement/ marriage?

Premediation

Although the aim of AIM is to get people who generally agree into alignment, it can also be used in more contentious situations. In the course of our personal and professional lives, we've occasionally had the need for legal and mediation help.

There are times when having a lawyer on your side and/or an impartial mediator between negotiations can feel like a godsend. For instance, when a child is involved in a divorce, it can feel like a Sisyphean task to keep things calm and productive.

Using AIM, either alone or with your counterpart, prior to a mediated conversation helps limit interactions to one topic at a time and sets the stage for mediation so that you (both) feel like it was productive and fair.

Keep in mind you're not figuring out the answers yet, just laying the groundwork for the meeting so compromises can be made while with the mediator. The examples below are focused on divorce agreements—something we both are quite familiar with from previous relationships—but can be easily modified to accommodate any kind of mediation.

- ▶ **Intentions:** I'd like to get clear on what this meeting is about so I can prepare. My intention for our meeting is to renegotiate the child-sharing schedule so we can avoid last-minute changes. What are your intentions for this meeting?
- ▶ **Concerns:** I want the schedule to feel fair to both of us as well as to our child. I'm concerned you'll feel I'm trying to get more than my 50 percent of time, but I do care that everyone feels good about this because it's best for our kid. I'm concerned that your travel schedule for work changes a lot during the week, leading to

last-minute switches during the school day. I'm also concerned about how we pay for after-school care if the number of days our child stays with one of us changes. What are your concerns related to the schedule?

▶ **Boundaries:** I'd like to keep this meeting to just the topic of scheduling our shared custodial time and related issues. Do you have any boundaries for this meeting?

▶ **Dreams:** What is your ideal outcome from the session?

Although this conversation can't guarantee that both parents will be mature and focus on the child's best interests, it can make issues clearer and start a precedent for what might otherwise be an off-the-rails, emotional meeting.

If face-to-face interactions aren't possible, either emotionally or geographically, feel free to email these questions or have the conversation over the phone. And if it is impossible to have a productive conversation without a mediator present, you can use the questions above simply to get clear by yourself before you walk into the mediation.

A New Home

Knowing specifically what you want is often half the battle in getting it. We find this especially true when it comes to finding and setting up a new home. Although it is easy to dream big (I want a big house on a couple of acres with a pool and a tennis court), the devil is often in the details and the underlying motivations (I want to live somewhere near nature that's good for gardening and entertaining).

When you get specific about what you want your home to do for you—what Bob calls the *design criteria*—you can get more creative about having it. Perhaps you don't need your own pool—which is not only expensive but time-consuming to maintain—but just want to live near one.

Our first home together was a row house in Brooklyn. We lived there for a few years and often talked of moving. But our place was cheap, large (by New York standards), and convenient to public transport. These factors, combined with a dread of moving, kept us stuck in our place—but it didn't keep us from talking about it a lot.

Eventually we began to use AIM to capture what we really wanted in a home, and we developed an increasingly clear picture of what home meant to us and what the minimum requirements were. Sometimes we challenged each other to be more realistic, like when Bob wanted four bedrooms so we each could have an office, but Alex pointed out that four-bedroom apartments in New York were rare and, therefore, expensive. We also challenged each other to be more ambitious, like when Alex said she was willing to live somewhere without garden access.

Because we talked in so much detail about what we wanted—and the underlying emotional and practical needs a home would give us—we were able to spot the right place with almost no effort. This is extremely rare in New York, where finding a home is often a legal, logistical, and interpersonal ordeal.

Here are some questions to get you going:

- ► **Intentions:** Why do you want to move? What do you want to be able to do in our new home? How do you want our home to feel?
- ► **Concerns:** What worries you about moving? What might go wrong with choosing a new place?
- ► **Boundaries:** How many bedrooms, bathrooms, and so on must our new home have and why? Where does it need to be physically in terms of school, shopping, transportation, and work? What must the new home *not* have? How much work are you willing to do on it? Is a fixer-upper okay, or would a smaller or less convenient place that requires less work be preferable?
- ► **Dreams:** It is a Sunday morning in our new place—what's happening and how do you feel? Now do the same for a Monday morning. You are having people come visit—describe how our new home works. We are bringing a new baby home—describe how our new home works for the baby as an infant, toddler, and young child. When, ideally, would we move out of our new home—never?

Home with Kids

Humans like some control over their lives. We believe that children want to feel respected and to have a safe way to begin to govern their own lives. We have been using variations of AIM with our son since he was five or six years old. In asking him clear, age-appropriate versions of the intentions, concerns, boundaries, and dreams prompts, we have helped him to find his voice, and we include his desires in events and decisions when possible.

We try to run our family as a democracy, but we are also clear that Mom and Bob are the ultimate dictators and can overrule certain dreams. After all, ice cream for breakfast, lunch, and dinner isn't a good idea. However, we can be flexible about when chores are completed and are able to offer more choices that suit everyone.

Here are some examples of how we use AIM with our son, and we hope they help you develop a new, inclusive way of communicating as a family:

Planning the School Year

Before middle school began, we took our son for a family brunch to celebrate the end of summer and connect about the upcoming year. To help us understand what he was feeling and to set expectations for a new school schedule, we used AIM after we had all eaten.

- **Intentions:** What do you hope to get out of seventh grade?
- **Concerns:** What are you worried about this year? What do you know about your new teachers? What do you think homework will be like this year? Are there other kids you worry about being around? What if there is trouble keeping up with a subject this year?
- **Boundaries:** What are you sure you want to experience or not experience this year? What are the screen-time rules during the week? What are the homework and grade expectations this year? How many after-school activities or sports are you considering this year?
- **Dreams:** If this turns out to be the best year ever, what will have happened? What do you hope to learn this year? How do you want to feel about yourself this year?

Selecting the Right School, Program, or Camp
Any step along your child's journey is a good opportunity to use AIM. Whether it's choosing a kindergarten, summer camp, high school, or college, checking in as a family team can alleviate stress and help share the responsibilities.

At the time we're writing this book, our son is just twelve years old. In New York, it's the age of the high-school applications gauntlet. As the largest public school system in the United States, this means the process is something akin to *Supermarket Sweep* meets *Hunger Games.*

To help us stay focused as we sift through the more than 700 high school programs, our family has used AIM several times in getting us to the finish line. Our conversations have focused on

- ▶ what kind of program our son wants to apply to (film and photography, fine arts, sciences, or other specialized programs),
- ▶ what kind of school he wants to attend (large public school with multiple programs, small and private school with a highly focused structure on one topic, etc.), and
- ▶ the possible commute (a subway ride to a school on the other side of the city could take more than an hour, one way).

We want our son to feel like he has a voice in the process, but we also don't want him to feel overwhelmed by it. He's young, and we don't want him to feel too much pressure too fast. Twelve years old is quite young to feel you are being judged as worthy or unworthy. AIM has been a useful guide when inviting his input:

- ▶ **Intentions:** What do you want to get out of your school or camp experience? What is important to you about a school?
- ▶ **Concerns:** What are you worried about when you think about high school or camp? What scares you about changing schools?

▶ **Boundaries:** What are you sure about when it comes to choosing a school or camp? What must the school you go to have in terms of clubs, subjects, sports, and so on? What are the deal breakers (e.g., if it doesn't have this, I'm not going; if it has this, I'm not going?)

▶ **Dreams:** Imagine yourself graduating from school in a few years, and you are looking back on a wonderful school experience. What happened during those years? What did you learn? What did you experience? Where are you going next?

Through these conversations, we've discovered what is ideal for our family and what's ideal for our son as an individual. We'll continue to have variations throughout the application process, and we'll be well prepared for when he's ready to apply to college (or take a "gap year," as we've recently discovered he's already thinking about—thanks, AIM!).

So Much More

Moving from an authoritarian "my way or the highway" type of relationship, AIM allows for a more democratic style of relating in which everyone has a say and all parties are included.

As you master the steps in one area of your life, you'll likely notice your communication becoming more effective in other areas as well. As you feel surer that you've covered all the important aspects of a topic, you'll likely feel more confident in yourself and your decisions. As others feel your care and respect for their thoughts and emotions, they'll likely feel more connected and cooperative with you and your shared goals. And that's what we mean by radical alignment.

We are sure there are many other circumstances in which AIM can be useful.

9

set up the all-in method so everyone wins

> "WELL BEGUN IS HALF DONE."
> —IRV GOWER (BOB'S DAD)

> "'ANGER IS USEFUL,' SAYS OUR ADVERSARY, 'BECAUSE IT MAKES MEN MORE READY TO FIGHT.' ACCORDING TO THAT MODE OF REASONING, THEN, DRUNKENNESS ALSO IS A GOOD THING, FOR IT MAKES MEN INSOLENT AND DARING, AND MANY USE THEIR WEAPONS BETTER WHEN THE WORSE FOR LIQUOR. . . . NO MAN BECOMES BRAVER THROUGH ANGER, EXCEPT ONE WHO WITHOUT ANGER WOULD NOT HAVE BEEN BRAVE AT ALL: ANGER DOES NOT THEREFORE COME TO ASSIST COURAGE, BUT TO TAKE ITS PLACE."
> —SENECA

No MATTER WHAT kind of connection you're trying to make with people, poor communication causes problems. Delays, hurt feelings, lack of trust, and general stress can all be linked to poorly run meetings and bad conversations.

Communication flows in both directions and requires being fully present and listening well. If we allow ourselves to "zone out" during an important conversation, we might miss body language that adds an important nuance or even indicates a red flag.

Have you ever been so hungry that you snapped at a friend or colleague? Has your blood sugar dropped, leaving your brain running at 50 percent, causing you to miss something important? Have you had a glass of wine or a beer and then said or done something you regretted later? Have you jumped to conclusions or been rude to a friend because you were angry about an earlier interaction?

You're not alone.

Being angry, hungry, and under the influence of alcohol are three common obstacles to smooth, respectful, productive communication. To ensure that your important conversations go well, you have to show up with your energy, focus, and awareness at full strength. As a health and success coach for more than fifteen years, Alex has firsthand experience with the ways in which nutrition, physiology, and neurology overlap.

AHA! Communication and Physiology

The twelve-step community uses an acronym for hungry, angry, lonely, or tired (HALT) to help those in recovery pause when they are in danger of making a bad decision. The idea is that if you are experiencing one or more of these states, you are perhaps not going to make the best decisions, and you should deal with these physical conditions first before doing anything rash.

In our work as coaches and facilitators, we've noticed a few similar common obstacles to good communication and staying present. And we've noticed that the same conditions impede real communication in our relationship as well. So, we have put in place an agreement to pause communication whenever we are angry (A), hungry (H), or have had alcohol (A)—even a single glass of wine. We use the acronym AHA as an easy way to remember.

Each of these states changes our physiology and psychology. Anger is a kind of intoxicant that we generate internally, hunger similarly alters our ability to think, and alcohol (or any intoxicant, including too much sugar) we consume will create a physiological and emotional impediment to being fully present.

We find it essential to avoid these when it comes to important group decisions. In our relationship, we have an explicit agreement that either of us can call a pause to any discussion and ask for an intermission while we calm down, eat, and or sober up. As Seneca says, "If you want to determine the nature of anything, entrust it to time: when the sea is stormy, you can see nothing clearly."

This is not always easy to hear when we're in the heat of the moment, but it always leads to a better outcome. Sometimes it means going to bed angry for one or both of us—which violates some common relationship advice—but we find that problems are easier to solve after we are well rested, and sometimes they even evaporate in the middle of the night.

We invite you to take notice. When you find yourself experiencing any of these three states, use it as an opportunity to hit pause, take care of your physical and emotional needs first, and then come back to the situation when you feel more centered. We also invite facilitators and participants to make sure they and everyone else are well rested, well fed, and not intoxicated during high-stakes conversations.

You might not have full control of emotional states such as anger and loneliness, but controlling the conditions you can will lead to better outcomes. Several years ago, Bob found himself going through a breakup and also unemployed. This was a difficult time in his life, and he noticed that he was frequently having emotional arguments with the woman who was becoming his ex.

Although Bob has never been a heavy drinker, he did notice that every bad argument had one common element—wine. He realized that he had some negative patterns of thinking and communication that came from childhood trauma and a history of depression.

While working with a therapist, he realized that clearing up his thinking and perceptions was essential, and alcohol was getting in the way. For the next few years, Bob was completely sober, and he committed to avoiding drama, meditated daily (he still does), and focused almost all his energy on finding work and then on doing the job after he found it.

These simple acts transformed Bob's cognition. Once plagued by depression, drama-filled relationships, self-doubt, and chronic financial insecurity, his life is now transformed. Although there are many contributing factors to this new turn of events, including the good luck of meeting Alex and having a successful consulting practice, his simple commitment to be a clear and good communicator made much of the difference.

Making sure you and your conversation partners are in good mental and physical shape will ensure better, more productive outcomes. Here is a breakdown of each element of AHA, a pause-worthy acronym, for the All-In Method (AIM).

ANGRY

Unexamined anger is like an unexploded bomb, just waiting to rip through your conversation. Although anger is a normal and healthy human emotion, you need to identify any existing anger and address it in a healthy way so that you don't bring it unintentionally to an important meeting.

Anger is perhaps the most acceptable emotion to express at work and is often far more socially acceptable than sadness or grief. We should note that this is mainly true for men, who are often viewed as powerful, committed, or passionate when they express anger. Women, in contrast, can be labeled hysterical or bitchy for similar behavior. And people of color of any gender are held to an entirely different standard when it comes to expressing anger in the workplace. Gender and racial dynamics aside, anger can be an important signal that your boundaries are being crossed, but when you express it, you might make others feel less safe and less trusting of you. In short, anger is extremely complicated.

Emotionality in the workplace and other relationships is an important topic. Although it is important to acknowledge our emotions, acting on them can be problematic. Anger, when not addressed or used skillfully, can derail communication because it can cause discomfort and withdrawal in others— remember our lessons on psychological safety and how easy it is to curtail someone's attempts to speak.

A helpful tool Bob uses to open most of his meetings is to ask everyone a question that has nothing to do with the meeting itself. This can help people bring their attention to the people there. Sometimes the question is simple: What has your attention? This creates an invitation to express and discharge anything else on your mind that is not the business at hand. It also creates an opportunity for empathy. If someone shares that their child is home sick, and the morning has been super hectic for them, we might be more generous if they appear impatient or distracted during the meeting.

Sometimes Bob uses questions designed to generate a specific mental and physical state: What are you looking forward to (that is not work)? This creates feelings of hope and optimism. What is the biggest risk you've ever taken? This one taps into courage and vulnerability.

Anger can cloud perceptions and limit our ability to see our situation clearly and therefore develop good solutions.

As the Dalai Lama says, "Anger may seem to be a source of energy, but it's blind. It causes us to lose our restraint. It may stir courage, but again it's blind courage."

Your AIM conversation might not be the place to bring up the origins of your anger, but it can be a venue for sharing the physical conditions anger or other emotions are causing in you. The design of AIM allows for emotions to be acknowledged; however, if you are feeling a particularly strong emotion, it is best for you to soothe yourself before attempting to discuss the inciting event.

It's not necessary, or even healthy, to bury anger. We encourage you to look at it, question its source, and use it as a possible signal that something important is happening. Here are a few ways you can work with your experience of anger or other intense emotions that can help you be present and engage productively.

Bring Awareness to Your Body
Describe the physical symptoms of anger and state your desire to be present. For example: I'm feeling tension in my neck, I am breathing shallowly, and I'm achy in my forehead, but I'm here and dedicated to being present.

Another way to manage your anger before a conversation is to give yourself a break and go for a vigorous walk or get some fresh air while stretching. Go to the bathroom and lock the door to do some pushups against the sink or do jumping jacks.

Bring Attention to Your Breathing

Go outside to your car or a private spot to breathe consciously and deeply. The four-seven-eight breathing pattern, developed by Andrew Weil, has been shown to calm the nervous system:

1. Sit down with your feet on the floor and your back straight.
2. First, breathe out through your mouth, exhaling completely.
3. Next, close your lips, inhaling silently through your nose as you count to four in your head.
4. Then hold your breath for seven seconds.
5. Exhale completely from your mouth for eight seconds.
6. Repeat three to five times.

You might be dealing with more systemic forms of anger that come from taking on too much in your life and work. Feeling overloaded and overwhelmed are almost universal conditions in the modern lives we are living. Use the boundary portion of AIM to create a new boundary that will protect your self-care. You could share that you have a boundary of not staying past 5:00 p.m. at work, not answering work emails on nights or weekends, or being committed to taking a vacation in the next two months.

You might also be rightfully angry or anxious because you're experiencing or witnessing racism, sexism, unethical actions, or microaggressions in your workplace. Can you express these as concerns using AIM? Can you frame it as a dream to have diversity and inclusion workshops added to your workplace?

If this brings attention to long-standing frustrations, anxiety, or anger-management issues, you deserve support. Inquire with your health insurance provider or human resources department to find out if therapy, acupuncture, medical massage, or other professional help is available. Sometimes anger feels like a constant state of being and could be connected to childhood trauma or personal issues.

HUNGRY

If your body is hungry, your brain is too.

When your brain is running low on fuel, your willpower, patience, focus, and decision-making are impaired. Your brain is your body's largest consumer of energy. When you begin to sense your blood sugar is low, know that your "brain sugar" is low too!

Willpower is your ability to control your emotions and actions and is easily affected by hunger. We each get a finite, or limited, amount of willpower every day, and hunger depletes the brain and body of this control. It's easy to lose your temper when your willpower is down, so check in with yourself: Are you hungry going into an important conversation?

Avoid eating sugary foods before or during important conversations. A sugar rush, followed by a crash, is a sure way to derail anyone's attention, willpower, and ability to be present.

Skip the cookies and sodas. Bring or provide low-sugar, high-protein snacks for longer meetings. Meats, cheeses, nuts, seeds, and other low-sugar snacks will have a less negative impact on your blood sugar ("brain sugar").

UNDER THE INFLUENCE OF ALCOHOL

When you drink alcohol, a whole host of physiological changes occurs. Although the pleasurable release of dopamine might seem like a way to add creativity or relaxation to a meeting, a host of negative consequences comes as a chaser with those drinks:

- ▶ Lowered inhibitions, leading to poor judgment
- ▶ Trouble concentrating and speaking
- ▶ Loss of physical coordination
- ▶ Dulled perception
- ▶ Impaired vision
- ▶ Mood swings

Alcohol increases the amount of norepinephrine, a stimulating neurotransmitter, in the brain. When norepinephrine is elevated, your inhibitions decrease and impulsiveness increases. This makes it harder to stay aware of the potential consequences of your actions and words.

Alcohol reduces the functions in your behavior-inhibition. This dangerous mix makes it harder for you to work out how you're feeling and how you think through potential consequences.

Your prefrontal cortex slows down when you drink alcohol. This is the part of your brain that helps you think rationally and clearly, truly an important factor in using AIM successfully. Decision-making and rational thinking are disrupted, and you're more likely to act without considering your actions first. Your sense of control over your emotions breaks down along with your willpower over aggressive thoughts and actions. It becomes harder to gauge when you've gone too far, and situations can get out of hand faster if you've been drinking.

Because alcohol acts like sugar in the body, remember that your "brain sugar" is affected by drinking.

In our marriage, if either of us has had even one glass of wine, and we get into a disagreement, we have an agreement that one of us can hit the proverbial pause button, and the conversation is tabled until the next day. It has served us well, and we decided to carry it into our consulting work, avoiding alcohol at retreats until the final send-off dinner.

May I See You Now?

Busyness is the most fashionable "disease" of the modern age. If you're a leader or executive, meetings take up five times as much of your calendar as they did in the 1960s. If you're a parent or part of a couple, you might rely on time in the car with kids to have important or intense conversations because your family is finally together in one place and unable to escape! Although we can't set your calendar boundaries for you, we do want to help your meetings be more effective.

Whenever possible and practical, we recommend having in-person meetings for AIM. This is by far the highest-resolution form of communication. But if that's not possible, then video is the best way to go, and, of course, ask people to be in a place that is quiet and distraction free.

Evidence shows that around 55 percent of communication is body language, whereas another 38 percent is tone of voice—seeing and hearing the person you're talking with makes a huge difference in creating the best outcomes for a virtual meeting.

Although we love using telecommunication platforms for video group meetings, not being physically together in the same room will make communication less powerful and effective. If you don't see the nonverbal cues, gestures, posture, and overall body language of the person you're communicating with, you might miss something important.

Remind everyone to look at the screen and the person speaking. As the speaker, do your best to watch the body language of the people listening to you.

Take a Break

Do you ever feel like your brain is full? Us too. Mental fatigue is real and happens after a prolonged period of thinking, talking, or any other kind of cognition. Basically, your brain gets sent into overdrive, leaving you feeling exhausted, sapping motivation and productivity, and killing your overall ability to think clearly.

When we gather for important conversations, it can be difficult to take a break, and many people try to muscle through the fatigue. Although this might be the right call at times, it is important to be aware of physiological limitations.

If you sit still for more than twenty minutes, there will be a measurable decrease in brain derived neurotrophic factor (BDNF), an important neurotransmitter. In other words, the longer we sit, the worse our brains work. Alex describes BDNF as "Miracle Gro for your brain," and the best way to get it flowing again is to move your body.

However, breaks can also interrupt the subtle and sensitive emotional tenor of the room. If you sense your energy or that of others in the room flagging, a quick, quiet break to stand up and stretch can work wonders for mental energy.

■ ■ ■ ■ ■

Although the suggestions and thoughts in this chapter will not ensure a perfect outcome to your conversation, you can, through self-awareness and preparation, create a higher likelihood that it will go well.

take flight

"MARRIAGE IS A HUMAN GROWTH MACHINE."
—DAVID SCHNARCH

"BE HONEST, FRANK, AND FEARLESS AND GET SOME GRASP
OF THE REAL VALUES OF LIFE. . . . READ SOME GOOD, HEAVY,
SERIOUS BOOKS JUST FOR DISCIPLINE: TAKE YOURSELF IN
HAND AND MASTER YOURSELF."
—W. E. B. DU BOIS

"NO MATTER YOUR AGE, YOUR BRAIN, LIKE YOUR MUSCLE,
GROWS (NEUROGENESIS AND NEUROPLASTICITY) THROUGH
NOVELTY AND NUTRITION, SO TRY SOMETHING NEW EACH DAY."
—JIM KWIK

WE RECOMMEND INTRODUCING the All-In Method (AIM)
with this idea: it is a beginning, not an end. All human interactions are opportunities for growth, change, and increased
self-knowledge.

As a couple, we have been using this conversation on and
off for years. You don't need to reach a final, unchanging
agreement on the first try! In fact, we recommend that you
look at this as a safe way to continue growing, changing, and
coming back together, again and again.

Some conversations we personally return to repeatedly. Dreams are especially fun to ask each other about. But we also find that we listen to each other differently now. Often, even in casual conversation, one of us will drop something that sounds like a concern, and the other will naturally ask to hear more about that.

As with musical skills, you must master the basics first so you can improvise later. AIM is a kind of deliberate practice—if you do it regularly and frequently, it will create more skill and ease in all of your communications.

Actively engaging in this kind of thoughtful communication resonates with people. Our deepest hope is that you feel more authentic, strong, and open to others as you practice AIM and that the people you invite into the process find the courage to do the same.

MASTERY

Although the focus of AIM is interacting with others, we find that the biggest impact of relationships are the opportunities they present for personal growth. In the chapter opening quote by David Schnarch, he notes that marriage is a growth machine—we'd say the same for friendships, work relationships, and relationships with family members.

We find it helpful to remember that often the most profound effects of interacting with others are in our relationship to ourselves. Learning to bring our best self to conversations is a lifelong practice. And sometimes we learn the most from the most challenging interactions.

But communication, like meditation, is a practice. The true value of meditation comes not from moments of sublime and effortless concentration but from developing the ability to return to focus when our attention wanders. The continual refocusing builds the muscle of attention in a meditation practice, and the same is true in focused interactions with others.

AIM is a practice. You will lose focus from time to time and find yourself disturbed or angry or upset and reeling after a conversation goes sideways. Conversations might even go terribly wrong from time to time—they certainly still do for us. However, the point is not to be perfect but to do your best, forgive yourself when you mess up, and commit to doing better the next time.

Our (Real) Intention for You

We are grateful you picked up this book—and made it this far through it! As we said in the introduction, our intention is that after reading this book you will be able to use AIM in high-stakes personal and professional interactions and perhaps even facilitate it for others. But this is just the starting place.

We humans are social creatures who find meaning, purpose, and agency in our lives primarily through our interactions and collaborations with others. Our real intention is that this simple tool might help you create better interactions and, therefore, better relationships and, therefore, a better and more impactful life.

We were fortunate to discover this tool, and it wasn't until we'd been using it for years that we realized how central it had become to our marriage and our work lives. It has contributed deeply to our feelings of resilience, purpose, joy, and impact. We hope it does the same for you.

appendix: cheat sheet

THE ALL-IN METHOD (AIM) is a simple, guided conversation that helps two or more people gain clarity and develop a deeper understanding of, and appreciation for, each other and their shared experience. It's useful whenever you are discussing a subject that feels important and is likely to raise deep emotions. AIM is constructive for making plans, creating agreements, and getting everyone on the same page in a successful way.

SET THE STAGE

Make sure you are in a comfortable, distraction-free space with plenty of time available to complete the conversation without feeling rushed.

Next, name the specific issue you will be discussing and why. A good setup will look like this: we are discussing Project X so we can become a great team—or, we are discussing our summer vacation so we both have a wonderful time.

Have the Conversation

Now it's time to have the conversation. Go one section at a time, and make sure you give each person ample time to dig deep and answer completely before moving on to the next person.

The questions below are prompts to get you thinking, so don't feel pressured to answer each one. Challenge yourself to speak with authenticity and to listen without judgment.

When speaking, do your best to be vulnerable and complete. When listening, be as open as possible. Only ask questions if they are encouraging and genuinely curious. Never ask questions that contain hidden judgments.

If there are three or more people in the conversation, have someone volunteer to be the facilitator. The facilitator's job is to keep the conversation moving in an orderly pattern and prevent crosstalk—feedback to someone on what they share—or excessive conversation.

Intentions
- ▶ Why do you want to be a part of this?
- ▶ Why are we doing this?
- ▶ How might this support your personal goals?
- ▶ What values of yours led you to get involved?

Concerns
- ▶ What worries you about the team, our plan, and so on?
- ▶ What do you think will get in our way?
- ▶ Where will we run into trouble?
- ▶ If this fails, why will it fail?

Boundaries
- ▶ What do you need to be at your personal best?
- ▶ What will keep us from overreaching or burning out?
- ▶ What rules or standards will help this team be the best?
- ▶ What must, or must not, change?

Dreams
- ▶ If this goes incredibly well, what will be true?
- ▶ How will you feel? Where will you be?
- ▶ What metrics will have shifted?
- ▶ You're looking back after a successful conclusion—what is true for you or others?

notes

CHAPTER 1

1. Gallup, 2018, "Employee Engagement on the Rise in the U.S."
2. Barbara Fredrickson, 2014, University of North Carolina School of Social Work.

CHAPTER 2

1. Associated Press, 2017, interview with Katharyn Hahn regarding Jill Soloway.
2. Steven Kotler and Jamie Wheal, 2018, *Stealing Fire: How Silicon Valley, the Navy SEALs, and Maverick Scientists Are Revolutionizing the Way We Live and Work* (New York: Dey Street).
3. Kotler and Wheal, *Stealing Fire.*
4. Samuel Stebbins, 2018, "A Look at the Highest and Lowest Paying Jobs of 2018," *USA Today.*
5. *New York Times,* 2016, "What Google Learned from Its Quest to Build a Perfect Team."
6. David Schnarch, 2011, *Intimacy and Desire: Awaken the Passion in Your Relationship* (Chicago, IL: Midpoint).
7. "What It's Like to Work at IDEO," medium.com/future-of-work/what-its-like-to-work-at-ideo-6ca2c961aae4.
8. Shane Snow, 2018, *Dream Teams: Working Together Without Falling Apart* (New York: Penguin).
9. Chris Voss, 2016, *Never Split the Difference: Negotiating as If Your Life Depended on It,* Kindle ed. (New York: Harper Collins), 52.

CHAPTER 3

1. en.wikibooks.org/wiki/Professionalism/Roger_Boisjoly,_Morton _Thiokol,_and_NASA.
2. Amy Edmonson, 2018, *The Fearless Organization,* (Hoboken, NJ: John Wiley and Sons).
3. Edmonson, *Fearless Organization.*
4. Priya Parker, 2018, *The Art of Gathering* (New York: Riverhead).

CHAPTER 7

1. Liz Fosslien and Molly West Duffy, 2019, *No Hard Feelings: The Secret Power of Embracing Emotions at Work* (New York: Penguin).
2. Stanley McChrystal, Tantum Collins, David Silverman, and Chris Fussell, 2015, *Team of Teams: New Rules of Engagement for a Complex World* (New York: Penguin).
3. Terry Real, *Scene on Radio,* "Men."

resources and further reading

THANK YOU for picking up this book and learning about this technique. We hope you find it as valuable as so many others have. If you feel inspired, we'd love to hear from you!

Below are some places you can go to deepen your communication practice and extend the value of the All-In Method (AIM) in your work and home life.

RESOURCES

For additional AIM resources, including

- ▶ training videos,
- ▶ team chartering instructions,
- ▶ a printable PDF of the cheat sheet,
- ▶ AIM presentation slides,
- ▶ scripts for different circumstances,
- ▶ and more, go to bobgower.com/radicalalignment or alexandrajamieson.com/radicalalignment.

Further Reading

We've been inspired by many other writers and practitioners over the years, and the work of many people informs our work. We stand on the shoulders of giants.

Below are some of our favorite books, articles, and other resources, some of which we've quoted or referred to in this book and all of which have informed our thinking on relationships, communication, and life.

For up-to-date listings, please visit the resource pages on our respective websites. Although our lists overlap, we also have divergent interests and perspectives.

Go to bobgower.com/radicalalignment or alexandrajamieson.com/radicalalignment.

Books

Brach, Tara. 2004. *Radical Acceptance: Embracing Your Life with the Heart of a Buddha.* New York: Bantam Books.

Brown, Adrienne Marie. 2017. *Emergent Strategy: Shaping Change, Changing Worlds.* Chico, CA: AK Press.

Brown, Brené. 2015. *Daring Greatly: How the Courage to Be Vulnerable Transforms the Way We Live, Love, Parent, and Lead.* New York: Avery.

Brown, Jennifer. 2019. *How to Be an Inclusive Leader: Your Role in Creating Cultures of Belonging Where Everyone Can Thrive.* Oakland, CA: Berrett-Koehler.

Chödrön, Pema. 2002. *When Things Fall Apart: Heart Advice for Difficult Times.* Boulder, CO: Shambhala.

Csikszentmihalyi, Mihaly. 2008. *Flow: The Psychology of Optimal Experience.* New York: Harper Collins.

Dignan, Aaron. 2019. *Brave New Work: Are You Ready to Reinvent Your Organization?* Kindle ed. New York: Penguin.

Edmonson, Amy. 2018. *The Fearless Organization.* Hoboken, NJ: John Wiley and Sons.

Fosslien, Liz, and Molly West Duffy. 2019. *No Hard Feelings: The Secret Power of Embracing Emotions at Work.* New York: Penguin.

Headlee, Celeste. 2017. *We Need to Talk: How to Have Conversations That Matter.* New York: Harper Collins.

Holiday, Ryan. 2014. *Obstacle Is the Way, Ego Is the Enemy,* and *Stillness Is the Key* (a three-part series on stoicism). New York: Penguin.

Hsieh, Tony. 2010. *Delivering Happiness: A Path to Profits, Passion, and Purpose.* New York: Grand Central.

Kotler, Steven, and Jamie Wheal. 2017. *Stealing Fire: How Silicon Valley, the Navy SEALs, and Maverick Scientists Are Revolutionizing the Way We Live and Work.* New York: Dey Street.

Lencioni, Patrick M. 2012. *The Advantage: Why Organizational Health Trumps Everything Else in Business.* Hoboken, NJ: Jossey-Bass/John Wiley and Sons.

McChrystal, Stanley, Tantum Collins, David Silverman, and Chris Fussell. 2015. *Team of Teams: New Rules of Engagement for a Complex World.* New York: Penguin.

McKeown, Greg. 2014. *Essentialism: The Disciplined Pursuit of Less.* New York: Currency/Crown.

Meadows, Donella H. 2008. *Thinking in Systems: A Primer.* White River Junction, VT: Chelsea Green.

Parker, Priya. 2018. *The Art of Gathering.* New York: Riverhead.

Pillay, Srinivasan S. 2017. *Tinker Dabble Doodle Try: Unlock the Power of the Unfocused Mind.* New York: Ballantine.

Pink, Daniel H. 2009. *Drive: The Surprising Truth About What Motivates Us.* New York: Riverhead.

Rushkoff, Doug. 2019. *Team Human.* New York: Norton.

Schnarch, David. 2009. *Intimacy and Desire: Awaken the Passion in Your Relationship.* Chicago, IL: Midpoint.

Seneca. 2019. *How to Keep Your Cool: An Ancient Guide to Anger Management*, translated by James S. Romm. Princeton, NJ: Princeton University Press.

Sheridan, Richard. 2013. *Joy, Inc.: How We Built a Workplace People Love.* New York: Penguin.

Snow, Shane. 2018. *Dream Teams: Working Together Without Falling Apart.* New York: Penguin.

Tabaka, Jean. 2006. *Collaboration Explained: Facilitation Skills for Software Project Leaders.* Boston: Addison-Wesley.

Theurer, Bridgette, and Heather O'Neill Jelks. 2015. *Missing Conversations: 9 Questions All Leaders Should Ask Themselves.* Scotts Valley, CA: CreateSpace.

Voss, Chris. 2016. *Never Split the Difference: Negotiating as If Your Life Depended on It.* New York: Harper Collins.

Wheatley, Margaret J. 2006. *Leadership and the New Science: Discovering Order in a Chaotic World.* Oakland, CA: Berrett-Koehler.

Articles

Brooks, David. "Students Learn from People They Love: Putting Relationship Quality at the Center of Education." https://www.nytimes.com/2019/01/17/opinion/learning-emotion-education.html

Cuddy, Amy J. C., Matthew Kohut, and John Neffinger. "Connect, Then Lead." https://hbr.org/2013/07/connect-then-lead

Charles Duhigg, "What Google Learned from Its Quest to Build the Perfect Team." https://www.nytimes.com/2016/02/28/magazine/what-google-learned-from-its-quest-to-build-the-perfect-team.html

Websites

Cognitive Edge with Dave Snowden. https://cognitive-edge.com/

Conversation Factory with Daniel Stillman. https://theconversationfactory.com/

about the authors

Alexandra (Alex) Jamieson

When driven, creative women want an integrated, artistic approach to leadership, business, and life coaching to build their vision of success, they go to Alexandra Jamieson.

Alex mentors creators, founders, and leaders on the rise to take aligned action using their strengths, values, intuition, and creative thinking to achieve success on their own terms.

In her five bestselling books, award-winning podcast "Her Rules Radio," and weekly writing, she explores success energetics, positive psychology, embodied leadership, entrepreneurship, and personal growth strategies so that her readers and clients can bring their unique voice and work to the world in the service of their souls and the world.

Alexandra is a watercolorist and loves to create wild art projects with her teenage son while listening to 1980s music.

Bob Gower

Bob is a consultant who helps organizations become future-ready—more effective now and able to scale into the future best version of themselves. He has worked with leaders at organizations from multinationals like Chanel, Ericsson, Ford, and GE to non-profits like New York Public Radio, the Studio Museum in Harlem, the Center for Responsive Politics, and the Wikimedia Foundation, as well as innovative technology companies like Spotify and numerous startups.

In 2017 he co-founded Ethical Ventures, a management consultancy dedicated to social enterprises. Their mission is to create a future where organizations that do well and do good are the rule, not the exception.

Bob is the author of, *Agile Business: A Leader's Guide to Harnessing Complexity* and *Radical Alignment: How to Have Game-Changing Conversations to Transform Your Business and Life* (Sounds True 2020). He is a sought-after speaker and teacher, having keynoted gatherings on four continents and lectured at Columbia University, NYU's Stern School of Management, and business innovation programs around the world.

Bob's work spans strategy, organization design, and team development and draws inspiration from psychology, philosophy, systems theory, complexity science, evolutionary biology, anthropology, and spiritual traditions. Follow him at bobgower.com

About Sounds True

Sounds True is a multimedia publisher whose mission is to inspire and support personal transformation and spiritual awakening. Founded in 1985 and located in Boulder, Colorado, we work with many of the leading spiritual teachers, thinkers, healers, and visionary artists of our time. We strive with every title to preserve the essential "living wisdom" of the author or artist. It is our goal to create products that not only provide information to a reader or listener but also embody the quality of a wisdom transmission.

For those seeking genuine transformation, Sounds True is your trusted partner. At SoundsTrue.com you will find a wealth of free resources to support your journey, including exclusive weekly audio interviews, free downloads, interactive learning tools, and other special savings on all our titles.

To learn more, please visit SoundsTrue.com/freegifts or call us toll-free at 800.333.9185.

sounds true
WAKING UP THE WORLD